635
GLORY

5-9601 111

THE
Glory
OF
THE
Garden

THE Glory OF THE Garden

EDITED BY KATHLEEN BRONZERT AND BRUCE SHERWIN

Illustrated by Roberta Rosenthal

Produced by The Philip Lief Group, Inc.

AVON BOOKS  NEW YORK

Our sincerest thanks to Karen Bronzert and
Dr. Margaret Stewart, whose help and support
was essential in nurturing this project.

THE GLORY OF THE GARDEN is an original publication of Avon Books. This work has never before appeared in book form.

AVON BOOKS
A division of
The Hearst Corporation
1350 Avenue of the Americas
New York, New York 10019

Copyright © 1993 by The Philip Lief Group, Inc.
Illustrations copyright © 1993 by Roberta Rosenthal
Published by arrangement with the Philip Lief Group, Inc.
Library of Congress Catalog Card Number: 92-97000
ISBN: 0-380-76854-2

First Avon Books Trade Printing: March 1993

AVON TRADEMARK REG. U.S. PAT. OFF. AND IN OTHER COUNTRIES, MARCA REGISTRADA, HECHO EN U.S.A.

Printed in the U.S.A.

ARC   10   9   8   7   6   5   4   3   2   1

Contents

Foreword

vii

Chapter 1

In Praise of Gardens

1

Chapter 2

Toil and Reward

47

Chapter 3

Garden Life

99

Chapter 4

Season's Cycle

129

Chapter 5

Wind and Weather

171

Chapter 6
A Patch of Land
191

Chapter 7
It Begins with a Seed
247

Author Index
295

Subject Index
303

Foreword

$\mathcal{T}$he pleasure of gardens, like the pleasure of ruins, is a universal phenomenon. What is that aspect of our nature, whatever our nation, that makes gardens so appealing? In my case, perhaps it was my parents' love of flowers and gardens that strengthened my own love of nature to the point of choosing natural history as a profession. My father, no matter how tired from tilling the fields in rural North Carolina, always had a little time left for his roses. My mother, exhausted from keeping the farmhouse going, always had time for her daffodils, tulips, irises, and peonies. I learned from her that when time is short, bulbs are best.

There have been times in my life when the going was rough. Somehow the cares drifted away when I could tend the flower beds. Whether it was the exercise of pulling the weeds that relieved my frustrations, or whether it was the anticipation of the beauty to come, I always felt better after time in the garden.

Nature is truly awesome. Some of our awe and fear of nature may be reduced by gathering bits of it into the "pretend" world of a garden, where we are, to some extent, in control. Whatever the reasons, the satisfactions of gardening are real.

Nations take gardening with different degrees of dedication. For me, the English deserve the prize for the most magnificent gardens. What I like about the English style of gardening is the somewhat relaxed form their gardens take. Beauty without absolute control. But in their effort to colonize the world, the settlers from England did not leave their gardens behind. In my travels to remote parts of the world, wherever the English have been, there were gardens, and the English passed on their traditions of gardening to the peoples they ruled. Great was my surprise, in the foggy heights of the Blue Mountains of Jamaica, or in the center of the Nyika Plateau in Malawi in east central Africa, to find remnants of once beautiful English gardens. The hummingbirds whirred about the foxgloves in Jamaica, while the sunbirds, with their long, curved bills, used the same varieties of English flowers in Malawi and the Drakensburg

Mountains of Natal. Birds know of no such separations as people impose on one another.

Maintaining a garden with the myriad of insects waiting to devour any living plant is not easy; the urge to have a garden is great in spite of the obstacles. When it comes to gardening, one must be willing to share with insects, slugs, rabbits, and nature's other creatures. Often the worst "pests" have been brought from other continents with the flowers we love so much.

Spring in upstate New York is cold and short. But as soon as the cold March days allow, we are searching our garden for the first green shoots of the daffodils. By the time those buds finally break into their golden splendor, they must be fatigued from having been looked at so many times as we urged them out of the ground. Likewise, in the fall we give our undivided attention to the last aster and goldenrod. Even blossoms of the hated knapweed and dandelion become precious jewels. What a pleasure to have some of the heathers showing their buds, with great confidence that they will be in blossom in the spring when winter snows melt.

The Glory of the Garden has captured the essence and the joys of gardening through this collection of quotations from people, famous and not so famous, throughout history who garden or who have expressed in writing their attitudes about gardens. You may find many of your attitudes expressed here. If not, you may now be inspired to write down your own feeling about gardens and gardening.

Dr. Margaret M. Stewart,
Distinguished Teaching Professor
Department of Biological Sciences
State University of New York at Albany, and
Vice Chair of the Board of Directors,
Eastern New York Chapter
The Nature Conservancy

Chapter 1
In Praise of Gardens

A modest garden contains, for those who
know how to look and wait, more instruction
than a library.

Henri Frederic Amiel
(1821–1881, Swiss philosopher, poet)

*L*ife begins the day you start a garden.

Chinese Proverb

*C*ome, let me kiss the falling, kiss at rise,
Thou in the garden, I in Paradise.

Anonymous

*G*ardens were before gardeners, and but some
hours after the earth.

Sir Thomas Browne, The Garden of Cyrus,
(1605–1682, English writer, scholar)

*O*nly the flower sanctifies the vase.

Robert Underwood Johnson
(1853–1937, American humorist)

1

*S*how me your garden and I shall tell you what you
are.

Alfred Austin,
The Garden that I Love
(1835–1913, English poet)

*F*irst look:
The garden moss stretches an emerald cloak
Shadowed by the kisses of the sleeping flowers.
Then shut your eyes:
Streams are singing about the feet of rose-trees.

Anonymous

*R*oses that down the alleys shine afar,
And open Jasmine-Muffled lattices,
And groups under the dreaming garden-trees,
And the full moon and the white evening star . . .

Matthew Arnold
(1822–1888, English poet)

*T*he English cottage garden has very soft, irregular
lines to its borders. The plants blend in with each
other. It looks as though it just grew there.

June Clark (gardener)

*I*t is in gardens that the greatest delight, mixed with
much profit, is to be found.

Asemius (Latin poet)

The garden, historically, is the place where all the senses are exploited. Not just the eye, but the ear—with water, with birds. And there is texture, too, in plants you long to touch.

William Howard Adams (farmer, lawyer, scholar)

Is it not a pleasant sight to behold a multitude of trees round about, in decent form and order, bespangled and gorgeously apparelled with green leaves, blooms and goodly fruits as with a rich robe of embroidered work, or as a hanging with some precious and costly jewels or pearls, the boughs ladened and burdened, bowing down to you and freely offering their ripe fruits as a large satisfaction of all your labours?

Ralph Austein,
A Treatise of Fruit Trees

The more one gardens, the more one learns; and the more one learns, the more one realizes how little one knows.

Vita Sackville-West
(1892–1962, English poet, novelist)

I have a garden of my own,
But so with roses overgrown,
And lilies, that you would it guess
To be a little wilderness.

Andrew Marvell,
"The Nymph Complaining for
the Death of Her Fawn"
(1621–1678, English poet)

... *O*ne plant in a tin can
may be a more helpful and inspiring garden
to some mind
Than a whole acre of lawn and flowers
may be to another ...

> *Liberty Hyde Bailey,*
> Garden Making; Suggestions for the
> Utilizing of Home Grounds
> *(1821–1841, horticulturist)*

*S*tint yourself, as you think good, in other things; but don't scruple freedom in brightening home. Gay furniture and a brilliant garden are a sight day by day, and make life blither.

> *Sir Thomas F. Buxton*
> *(1786–1845, writer)*

*T*he glorious fragrance of blooming plants is one of the greatest (and sometimes overlooked) joys a garden can give.

> *Lee Bailey,* Country Flowers
> *(twentieth-century cookbook writer,*
> *home furnishings expert)*

*G*ardening is an art form, but it has lost its sense of history.

> *William Howard Adams (farmer, lawyer, scholar)*

My house is burned,
but the cherry tree in my garden
scatters its blossoms
as if nothing had happened.

Haiku by Bashō
(1644–1694, Oriental poet)

Gardens are our link with the divine.

William Howard Adams
(farmer, lawyer, scholar)

It gives one a sudden start in going down a barren, stony street, to see upon a narrow strip of grass, just within the iron fence, the radiant dandelion, shining in the grass, like a spark dropped from the sun.

Henry Ward Beecher
(1813–1887, American clergyman and writer)

Who loves a garden loves a greenhouse too.

William Cowper
(1731–1800, poet)

I love old gardens best—
tired old gardens
that rest in the sun.

Henry Bellaman (poet)

*A*ll that in this delightful garden grows,
Should happy be, and have immortal bliss.

Edmund Spenser, The Fairie Queene
(1552 or 1553–1599, English poet)

*P*lanning a garden in a restricted place is tanta-
mount to planning a small kitchen. It's much more
difficult than laying out a big one.

John Brookes
(English landscape designer)

These are the gardens of the desert, these
The unshorn fields, boundless and beautiful,
For which the speech of England has no name—
The prairies.

William Cullen Bryant,
"The Prairies"
(1794–1878, American poet)

A garden is a lovesome thing, God wot!

Thomas Edward Brown, "My Garden"
(1830–1897, British poet)

The ancients venially delighted in flourishing
gardens.

Sir Thomas Browne
(1605–1682, English writer, scholar)

Since I have been here, the deserted garden, planted
with large pines beneath which grows the grass, tall
and unkempt and mixed with various weeds, has suf-
ficed for my work and I have not yet gone outside . . .
By staying here, the doctor will naturally be better
able to see what is wrong and will be, I hope, more
reassured as to my being allowed to paint.

Vincent Van Gogh, 1853–1890,
letter from St. Remy, France,
to his brother, Theo
May 25, 1889 (Dutch painter)

*H*ere's the garden she walked across,
Arm in arm, such a short while since:
Hark, now I push it wicket, the moss
Hinders the hinges and makes them wince!

Robert Browning
(1812–1889, English poet)

*T*hey always called it Magic and indeed it seemed
like it in the months that followed—the wonderful
months—the radiant months—the amazing ones. Oh!
the things which happened in that garden! If you have
never had a garden you cannot understand, and if you
have had a garden you will know that it would take a
whole book to describe all that came to pass there.

Frances Hodgson Burnett,
1894–1924,
The Secret Garden

I am in a public garden, quite close to the street of
the pretty ladies, and Mourier for instance would
hardly enter it, although almost daily we walk in the
gardens, but on the other side . . . this side of the garden is also, for the same reason of chastity or morality,
destitute of any flowering bushes such as oleanders.
There are ordinary plain trees, pines in stiff clumps, a
weeping tree, and the green grass. But it is all so inti-
mate. Manet has gardens like this.

Vincent Van Gogh, 1853–1890,
letter from Arles, France,
to his brother, Theo
in 1888 (Dutch painter)

*D*aisies and buttercups, lo, they surpass coined gold of Kings.

Sir Richard Francis Burton
(1821–1890, English explorer, writer)

*M*en but make monuments of sin
Who walk the earth's ambitious round;
Thous hast the richer realm within
This garden ground.

Alice Brown,
"A Benedictine Garden"
(1856–1948, poet, novelist)

*T*here is a garden in her face
Where roses and white lilies grow;
A heavenly paradise is that place
Wherein all pleasant fruits do flow.
There cherries grow which none may buy,
Till "cherry-ripe" themselves do cry.

Thomas Campion,
"The Fourth Book of ARS"
(1567–1620, English poet)

*I*n old green gardens, hidden away
From sight of revel and sound of strife . . .
Here may I live what life I please,
Married and buried out of sight.

Violet Fane,
"In Old Green Gardens"
(1843–1905, poet)

$\mathcal{L}$et no one think that real gardening is a bucolic and meditative occupation. It is an insatiable passion, like everything else to which a man gives his heart.

Karel Čapek
(1890–1938, garden writer)

$\mathcal{T}$he market is the best garden.

George Herbert,
"Jacula Prudentum"
(1593–1633, poet)

$\mathcal{T}$hough I've wandered along many a shady lane, and down several primrose paths, I can't pretend to know much about gardening.

Truman Capote, Foreword,
First Garden,
by C. Z. Guest

$\mathcal{N}$ature—wild Nature—dwells in gardens just as she dwells in the tangled woods, in the deeps of the sea, and on the heights of the mountains; and the wilder the garden, the more you will see of her there. If you would see her unspoiled and in many forms, let your garden be a wild place, a place of trees and shrubs and vines and grass, even a place where weeds are granted a certain tolerance, for gardens which are merely spick and span plots of combed and curried flower-beds have little attraction for the birds or for the other people of the wild.

Herbert Ravenel Sass,
Adventures in Green Places

*W*hat is heaven? Is it not
Just a friendly garden plot.

William Bliss Carman
(1861–1929, American poet)

*T*ry to keep a garden beautiful to yourself alone and
see what happens—the neighbor, hurrying by to catch
his train of mornings, will stop to snatch a glimpse of
joy from iris purpling by your doorstep. The motorist
will throw on brakes and back downhill just to see
those Oriental poppies massed against the wall.
Nature is always on the side of the public.

Richardson Wright (garden writer)

A garden saw I, full of blossomy bows,
Upon a river, in a green meadow,
There as that sweetness evermore and now is,
With flowers white, blue, yellow, and red;
And cold well-streams, nothing did,
That swommen full of small Fishes light,
With fins red and scales silver-bright.

Geoffrey Chaucer
(1342–1400, English poet)

*T*he innocent must be counseled before tasting of
the pleasures a city garden brings: a refuge from a
world of troubles, an oasis where waters truly heal.

Linda Yang,
The City Gardener's Handbook
1990 (garden columnist)

*I*f you would be happy for a week,
 take a wife;
If you would be happy for a month,
 kill your pig;
But if you would be happy all your life,
 plant a garden.

Chinese proverb

. . . *T*he Japanese preference for small "scenes" and
the meditative approach to Zen Buddhism, combined
effortlessly to produce small landscaped "gardens"
that could offer some relief and peace of mind to
counter the effects of high-density living and bring
into the urban something of the mountains and their
spaces and serenity. Gardens were symbolic of this
greater outside; people could contemplate them and
regain some perspective on life; they could enter a different mood for a while, depending on the kind of
miniaturized scene they chose to construct.

A. K. Davidson,
The Art of Zen Gardens, 1983

*H*orticultural excellence in the garden can never
compensate for a fundamentally bad layout.

Thomas D. Church,
Gardens Are for People
1983 (landscape architect)

I have noticed the almost selfish passion for their
flowers which old gardeners have, and their reluc-
tance to part with a leaf or a blossom from their family. They love the flowers for themselves.

Charles Dudley Warner
(1829–1900, American novelist, essayist)

12

$\mathcal{G}$ardening is about cheating, about persuading unlikely plants to survive in unlikely places and when that trick is well accomplished the results can be highly satisfying.

David Wheeler, Hortus, *1992*

$\mathcal{E}$ven the term "garden" has changed its meaning. A garden used to have a horticultural meaning—a place where plants were grown to be displayed for mass effects or to be examined individually. It was a place to walk through, to sit in briefly while you contemplated the wonders of nature before you returned to the civilized safety of the indoors . . . The new kind of garden is still supposed to be looked at, but that is no longer its only function. It is designed primarily for living, as an adjunct to the functions of the house. How well it provides for the many types of living that can be carried on outdoors is the new standard by which we judge a garden.

Thomas D. Church,
Gardens Are for People
1983 (landscape architect)

$\mathcal{A}$ morning glory at my window satisfies me more than the metaphysics of books.

Walt Whitman, "Song of Myself"
(1819–1892, American poet)

$\mathcal{O}$ne of the rewards of buying an old house is the unexpected pleasure of uncovering the treasures which may be buried in the garden . . . full-grown boxwood hedges, and urns . . .

Thomas D. Church,
Gardens Are for People
1983 (landscape architect)

*I*n my mother's garden were green-leaved hiding-places, Nooks between the lilacs—oh, a pleasant place to play!

Margaret Widdemer (garden columnist)

A little garden not too fine,
Inclose with painted pales;
And woodbines, round the lot of twine,
Pin to the walls with nails.

John Clare
(1793–1864, English poet)

*I*n his garden every man may be his own artist without apology or explanation.

Louise Beebe Wilder,
Color in My Garden 1990

*N*o more I spake, but thanked kind fate,
When Idleness the garden gate
Threw open wide, and unafraid
To that sweet spot quick entry made.

W. Lorns and J. Clopinel
(thirteenth century poets)

*T*he old, old lady,
that nobody knows,
Sits in The Garden
Shelter, and sews.

Humbert Wolfe
(1886–1940,
English poet)

*M*y own philosophy about gardens is that they should have diversity, a happy mixture of strong design and careless rapture.

Rosemary Verey
(garden writer)

*W*ithin the garden there is healthfulness.

Emile Verhaeren
(1855–1916, writer)

... *E*re I descend to the grave
May I a small house and large garden have!
And a few friends, and many books, both true,
Both wise, and both delightful too!

Abraham Cowley
(1618–1667, English poet)

I pushed the gate that swings so silently,
And I was in the garden and aware
Of early daylight on the flowers there
And cups of dew sun-kindled.

Paul Verlaine
(1844–1896, poet)

*G*od the first garden made, and the first city Cain.

Abraham Cowley,
"The Garden"
(1618–1667, English poet)

15

*T*he imaginative gardener can turn a bit of ground that presents a special problem into a special delight.

Josephine Von Miklos, 1900–1972, and Evelyn Fiore,
The History, the Beauty, the Riches
of the Gardener's World

*M*ay your garden, like mine, give you "Victory" over the high cost of fresh vegetables as well as the joy and good health that come from living close to nature.

Jim Crocket, "Crocket's Victory Garden"
(1915–1979, garden expert, PBS-TV series host)

*M*aking a garden is an act of creation. It is man working with nature instead of against it . . .

Josephine Von Miklos, 1900–1972, and Evelyn Fiore,
The History, the Beauty, the Riches
of the Gardener's World

*G*ardens are the link between men and the world in which they live, for men in every age have felt the need to reconcile themselves with their surroundings and have created gardens to satisfy their ideals and aspirations.

Sylvia Crowe,
Garden Design, *1986*

*M*ore grows in the garden than the gardener has sown.

Unknown

*O*ne should learn also to enjoy the neighbor's garden, however small; the roses struggling over the fence, the scent of lilacs drifting across the road.

Henry Van Dyke
(1852–1933, American minister, writer)

*O*ne of the pleasures of being a gardener comes from the enjoyment you get looking at other people's yards.

Thalassa Cruso,
To Everything There Is a Season
(b. 1909, English horticulturist, writer)

. . . *G*ardening has been an art for several millennia, and our desire to make gardens comes also from a love of beauty—a desire to shape unruly nature into forms that please use more, from the hanging Gardens of Babylon to the White House Rose Garden.

Barbara Damrosch,
Theme Gardens
1982 (American landscape designer)

*W*hen skies are blue and days are bright
A kitchen-garden's my delight,
Set round with rows of decent box
And blowsy girls of hollyhocks.

Katharine Tynan
(1861–1931, Irish poet, novelist)

*T*he rose, wherein, the word divine makes itself flesh.

Dante (1265–1321, Italian poet)

17

*A*s gardening has been the inclination of kings and the choice of philosophers, so it has been the common favourite of public and private men . . .

Sir William Temple
(1628–1699, English statesman, essayist)

*'T*was a very small garden,
The paths were of stone,
Scattered with leaves,
With moss overgrown;
And a little old Cupid
Stood under a tree,
With a small broken bow
He stood aiming at me.

Walter De la Mare
(1873–1956,
English writer, anthropologist)

*T*he most exquisite delights of sense are pursued in the contrivance and planning of gardens, which with fruit, flowers, shades, fountains and the music of birds that frequents such happy places, seem to furnish all the pleasures of the several senses, and with the greatest, or at least the most natural perfections.

Sir William Temple, Miscellanea
(1628–1699, English statesman, essayist)

*W*hen I'm in my garden, or making flower preparations I often feel calm and at ease. For these reasons I like to use flowers in visualizations. Their images help me to reduce tension and experience deep relaxation.

Denise Diamond,
Living with Flowers

A small garden has great appeal beyond the charm of the flowers there. Smallness makes it personal, a private sanctuary with you in charge, here to shut out the world, its racing schedules, frustrations, and demands.

Rhoda Specht Tarantino,
Small Gardens Are More Fun

*I*t is good to be alone in a garden at dawn or dark so that all its shy presences may haunt you and possess you in a reverie of suspended thought.

James Douglas (writer)

*B*ut for me, the garden is not just a place to grow things. It is wonderful, of course, to have a piece of land on which one can propagate trees, berries, flowers and vegetables for one's own use and the enjoyment of others. But a garden is also a place where one can walk and think, sit and contemplate. A garden should have surprises, and should offer solace.

Martha Stewart,
Martha Stewart's Gardening Month by Month, *1991*
(American life-style writer, magazine editor)

*T*here can, however, scarcely be a more beautiful display of the art of the horticulturist, than a fine row of trained trees, their branches arranged with the utmost symmetry and regularity, and covered, in the fruits of the season, with large and richly coloured fruit.

Andrew Jackson Downing,
1815–1852,
Fruits and Fruit Trees of America

*G*ardening, in all its diversity, is America's most popular outdoor activity, so there is some foundation to my belief that if I don't get my order in to Roses of Yesterday and Today in a timely fashion, someone else will receive the 'Heinrich Munch' pink cabbage roses that I so much need in the perennial border.

Martha Stewart,
Martha Stewart's Gardening Month by Month, *1991*
(American life-style writer, magazine editor)

*I*f you once loved a garden
That love will stay with you.

Louise Driscoll

*G*ardening is not only the 'purest of human pleasures', but in this age it has come to be one of the most popular.

Sylvia Spencer (writer)

*T*he front yard was never a garden of pleasure; children could not play in these precious little enclosed plots, and never could pick the flowers—front yard and flowers were both too much respected. Only formal visitors entered therein, visitors who opened the gate and closed it carefully behind them, and knocked slowly with the brass knocker, and were ushered in through the ceremonious front door and the little ill-contrived entry, to the stiff foreroom or parlor.

Alice Morse Earle,
1851–1911, Old Time Gardens

I do not like gardening, nor am I particularly interested in gardens—in country gardens, that is to say. A town garden is a very different thing. It breaks up the bricks and mortar and provides a refuge from them for the town dweller.

Sheila Kaye Smith
(1887–1956, writer)

*T*hat sort of beauty which is called natural, as of vines, plants, trees, etc., consists of a very complicated harmony; and all the natural motions, and tendencies, and figures of bodies in the universe are done according to proportion, and therein is their beauty.

Jonathan Edwards
(1703–1758, American clergyman, philosopher)

*G*ardening is a habit of which I hope never to be cured, one shared with an array of fascinating people who helped me grow and bloom among my flowers.

Martha Smith,
Beds I Have Known, 1990

*T*his [garden] place is dedicated to the honorable pleasures of rejoicing the eye, refreshing the nose, and renewing the spirit.

Desiderius Erasmus,
Convivium Religiosum
(1466–1536, Dutch scholar, philosopher)

*T*he cottage garden; most for use designed, yet not of beauty destitute.

Charlotte Smith (English poet, novelist)

*M*y garden is a forest ledge
Which older forests bound;
The banks slope down to the blue lake-edge,
Then plunge to depths profound.

Ralph Waldo Emerson
(1803–1882, American writer, philosopher)

*W*hen I walk out of my house into my garden I walk out of my habitual self, my every-day thoughts, my customariness of joy or sorrow by which I recognize and assure myself of my own identity. These I leave behind me for a time, as the bather leaves his garments on the beach.

Alexander Smith (1830–1867, Scottish poet)

I have never had so many good ideas day after day as when I worked in the garden.

John Erskine (American writer)

*M*y garden, with its silence and the pulses of fragrance that come and go on the airy undulations, affects me like sweet music. Care stops at the gates, and gazes at me wistfully through the bars. Among my flowers and trees, Nature takes me into her own hands, and I breathe as freely as the first man.

Alexander Smith
(1830–1867, Scottish poet)

*O*ur blessed Saviour chose the garden For his Oratory, and dying For the place of his sepulcher.

John Evelyn
(1620–1706, English diarist)

*W*here there is one Englishman there is a garden. Where there are two Englishmen there will be a club. But that does not mean any falling off in the number of gardens. There will be three. The club will have one, too.

A. W. Smith (writer)

*M*e thinks I am in prison. Here be no galleries, no gardens to walk in.

King Edward VI
(1537–1553, English monarch)

*T*o make a great garden, one must have a great idea or a great opportunity.

Sir George Sitwell,
1860–1943,
On the Making of Gardens

*W*hat a desolate place would be a world without flowers?—It would be a face without a smile; a feast without a welcome.—Are not flowers the stars of the earth? And are not our stars the flowers of heaven?

Clara L. Balfour

The works of a person that builds begin immediately to decay; while those of him who plants begin directly to improve. In this, planting promises a more lasting pleasure than building.

William Shenstone
(1714–1763, English poet)

The flowering plants are often spoken of as the most advanced form of plant life, with the blossom itself as the evidence. In this sense, the flowering plant is the plant world's equivalent of the mammal in the animal world.

Hal Borland, 1900–1978,
Hal Borland's Book of Days

The best place to seek God is in a garden. You can dig for him there.

George Bernard Shaw, 1856–1950,
Adventures of the Black Girl in Her Search for God

In green old gardens, hidden away
From sight of revel and sound of strife;—
Here have I leisure to breathe and move,
And to do my work in a nobler way.

Violet Fane (1843–1905, poet)

Gardening is the only unquestionably useful job.

George Bernard Shaw
(1856–1950, Irish dramatist)

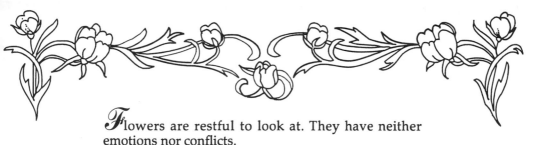

*F*lowers are restful to look at. They have neither emotions nor conflicts.

Sigmund Freud
(1856–1939, psychiatrist)

'*T*is this provides the body healthful foods,
And gives the tiller oft its varied yield—
Delicious greens and many kinds of herbs,
The sheen of grapes and fruitage rich of trees.

Aulus Septimius Serenus (poet)

*T*he purpose of agriculture is not the production of food, but the perfection of human beings.

Masanobu Fukuonoka,
Organic Gardening Magazine,
May/June 1991

$\mathcal{A}$ garden is a master of what a French writer calls the charming art of touching up the truth.

John Sedding (writer)

$\mathcal{A}$ good garden may have some weeds.

Thomas Fuller, M.D.
(1608–1661, American medical doctor, writer)

$\mathcal{N}$othing is more completely the child of art than a garden.

Sir Walter Scott
(1771–1832, Scottish novelist, poet)

$\mathcal{T}$here are fairies at the bottom of our garden!

Rose Fyleman, "The Fairies"
(1877–1957, English writer)

$\mathcal{A}$ garden is a delight to the eye, and a solace to the soul; it soothes angry passions, and produces that pleasure which is a foretaste of paradise.

Sadi
(1213–1292, Persian poet)

$\mathcal{T}$oday more and more gardeners have come to know the joys of plant sculpture, enthusiastically choosing from a rich variety of historic and modern styles.

Barbara Gallup and Deborah Reich,
The Complete Book of Totally Topiary
1988 (horticulturists)

I hold that everything that is beautiful should be sought for and studied in a garden.

> *Frank Galsworthy,*
> *in* Flower Grouping,
> *by M. Waterfield (1907)*

A garden is a garden is a garden.

> *Agnes Rothery (poet)*

*T*he true gardener, fickle lover that he is, should grow as many roses as he can find space for, that he may wander as the mood will take him, here and there from rose to rose, and in happy moments of imagination feast on a very nectar and ambrosia of scent and vision, and take his fill of happiness.

> *Frank Galsworthy,*
> *in* Flower Grouping,
> *by M. Waterfield (1907)*

*B*eing in a garden should be like being inside a piece of hollow sculpture.

> *James C. Rose (garden writer)*

*A*nd the Lord God planted a garden eastward in Eden.

> *Genesis 2:8*

A garden is an experience.

> *James C. Rose,*
> Creative Gardens

27

*W*ho would look dangerously up at planets, that might safely look downe at plants?

John Gerard
(1545–1612, garden writer)

*T*he greatest gift of a garden is the restoration of the five senses.

Hanna Rion,
Let's Make a Flower Garden

*T*he excellent art of . . . gardening hath been a study for the wisest, and exercise for the robust, a pastime for the best.

John Gerard
(1545–1612, garden writer)

*G*arden making is creative work, just as much as painting or writing a poem. It is a personal expression of self, an individual conception of beauty. I should as soon think of asking a secretary to write my book, or the cook to assist in a water color painting, as to permit a gardener to plant or dig among my flowers.

Hanna Rion,
Let's Make a Flower Garden

O, what delights to us the garden ground doth bring? Seed, leaf, flower, fruit, herb, bee, and tree, and more than I may sing.

Nicholas Grimaed (poet)

*C*ome—for at twilight are the garden hours
Of fragrant blossom, leaf, and dewy shade;
Among the close-clipped hedges, where is laid
The narrow graveled pathway, edged with flowers.

Henri De Regnier
(1864–1936, poet)

*G*ardening is the best therapy in the world. You can put so much into it and get so much back. Love is everything . . . How lucky we are to live on this beautiful earth—you can bring the beauty to yourselves through gardening.

C. Z. Guest,
First Garden
(1924–1984, socialite)

*Y*ear after year, from dusk to dusk,
How sweet this English garden grows,
Steeped in two centuries' Sun and musk,
Walled from the world in gray repose,
Harbor of honey—freighted bees,
And wealthy with the rose.

Lizette Woodworth Reese
(1856–1953, American poet)

*T*his is a living breathing garden.
Enter its beauty in aire—
And let its meaning of life surround you.
May your thoughts be as beautiful as what you behold.

Robert Gundacker, from a plaque
at a garden's entrance (garden expert)

A garden without shrubs is like a stage without the star performers—all the props are there, as well as the supporting cast, but the main actors who give weight and substance to the play have not appeared.

Reader's Digest
Guide to Creative Gardening, *1987*

*T*he kiss of the sun for pardon
The song of the birds for mirth—
One is nearer God's heart in a garden
Than anywhere else on earth.

Dorothy Gurney (English poet)

*I*nto your garden you can walk
And with each plant and flower talk;
View all their glories, from each one
Raise some rare meditation.

John Ray
(1627–1705, English naturalist)

*I*f I can someday see M. Claude Monet's garden, I feel sure that I shall see something that is not so much a garden of flower as of colors and tones . . . one that achieves an effect not entirely nature's, because it was planted so that only the flowers with matching colors will bloom at the same time, harmonized in an infinite stretch of blue or pink.

Marcel Proust
(1871–1922, writer, philosopher)

$\mathcal{A}$s for our love of gardens, it is the last refuge of art in the minds and soul of many Englishmen: if we did not care for gardens, I hardly know what in the way of beauty we should care for.

Sir Arthur Halpi (writer)

$\mathcal{H}$orticulture is, next to music, the most sensitive of the fine arts. Properly allied to Architecture, garden-making is as near as a man may get to the Divine functions.

Maurice Hewlett
(1861–1923, writer)

*W*hen at last I took the time to look into the heart of a flower, it opened up a whole new world—a world where every country walk would be an adventure, where every garden would become an enchanted one, where one could never again be lonely, bored or indifferent.

Princess Grace of Monaco,
My Book of Flowers
(1929–1982, Grace Kelly)

*Y*es! in the poor man's garden grow,
    Far more than herbs and flowers,
Kind thoughts, contentment, peace of mind,
    And joy for weary hours.

Mary Howitt (English writer)

. . . *I* created the Garden Club of Monaco. Now with this experience behind me, I feel that every city, every town, every village should have a garden club. It is as necessary for the lifeblood of a community as a library, art gallery, museum, and horticultural societies.

Princess Grace of Monaco,
My Book of Flowers
(1929–1982, Grace Kelly)

*A*s every gardener knows this immobility of plants does not seem to be much of an impediment—they will arrive rapidly enough on any bare patch of soil!

Anthony Huxley,
Green Inheritance
(botanist)

The whole plantation, the garden, and the rest prove that a man born with natural taste may guess at beauty without having ever seen its model. The General has never left America; but when one sees his house and his home and his garden it seems as if he had copied the best samples of the grand old homesteads of England.

A Polish visitor to Mount Vernon, June 1798

The gardens of the world are a treasure house of botanical skill, the creation of generations of individuals with a gift for beauty, rarity, and understanding of plants.

Anthony Huxley,
Green Inheritance
(botanist)

Just as people forced to do their own cooking turned ultimately to sophisticated foreign sources and became experts at techniques undreamed of by their mothers, so may American gardeners come to hanker after the horticultural arts unknown to earlier generations.

Eleanor Perenyi,
Green Thoughts: A Writer in the Garden, *1983*

Now was there made, fast by the Towers wall,
A garden fair, and in the corners set
An arbour green, with wandes long and small
Railed about . . .

King James I
(1394–1437 English monarch)

*I*t's a special treat to walk by a colorful front yard on a busy street, or to peek through a gate and enjoy a glimpse of a carefully tended patio or balcony terrace. There's nothing quite like a flourishing garden in a sea of concrete and glass.

> *Jane G. Pepper, Foreword,*
> *The City Gardener's Handbook, 1990,*
> *by Linda Yang*
> *(president, Pennsylvania Horticultural Society)*

*H*er gardens—how should any but herself Number? or know the blossoms growing there?

> *Robinson Jeffers*
> *(1887–1962, poet)*

I like the gardens with good bones and affirmed underlying structure . . . well-marked paths, well-built walls, well-defined changes in level.

> *Russell Page*
> *(1906–1985, American essayist)*

I am still devoted to the garden. But although an old man I am but a young gardener.

> *Thomas Jefferson*
> *(1743–1826, American president)*

*N*o occupation is so delightful to me as the culture of the earth, and no culture comparable to that of the garden.

> *Thomas Jefferson*
> *(1743–1826, American president)*

The word "garden" comes from the Hebrew and means "a pleasant place," and it is to this Eden that each gardener, after his or her fashion, strives to return.

George Ordish, 1908–1991,
The Living Garden

My garden will never make me famous,
I'm a horticultural ignoramus,
I can't even tell a stringbean from a soybean,
Or even a girl bean from a boy bean.

Ogden Nash
(1902–1971, American humorist)

The garden should fit its master or his tastes, just as his clothes do; it should be neither too large nor too small, but just as comfortable . . .

Gertrude Jekyll
(garden writer)

I know a little garden close,
Set thick with lily and red rose,
Where I would wander if I might
From dewy morn to dewy night.

William Morris,
"The Life and Death of Jason"
(1834–1896, English poet, artist)
A Garden by the Sea, St. I

*L*ittle strips in front of roadside cottages have a simple and tender charm that one may look for in vain in gardens of greater pretension.

Gertrude Jekyll
(garden writer)

*F*orget the spreading of the hideous town;
Think rather of the pack-horse on the down,
And dream of London, small and white and clean,
The clear Thames bordered by its gardens green.

William Morris
(1834–1896, English poet, artist)

*W*hen I was a child, I was very much alone, and nearly always in my playtime found my own amusement in the garden and shrubbery.

Gertrude Jekyll,
Children and Gardens, 1982

*A*nd now to sum up as to a garden. Large or small, it should look both orderly and rich. It should be well fenced from the outside world. It should by no means imitate either the willfulness or the wildness of nature, but should look like a thing never to be seen except near a house. It should, in fact, look like a part of the house.

William Morris
(1834–1896, English poet, artist)

The size of a garden has very little to do with its merit. It is merely an accident relating to the circumstances of the owner. It is the size of his heart and brain and goodwill that will make his garden either delightful or dull, as the case may be, and either leave it at the monotonous dead level, or raise it, in whatever degree he may, towards that of a work of fine art.

Gertrude Jekyll,
Wood and Garden, 1984

There are few of us who cannot remember a front yard garden which seemed to us a very paradise in childhood. Whether the house was a fine one and the enclosure spacious, or whether it was a small house with only a narrow bit of ground in front, the yard was kept with care, and was different from the rest of the land altogether.

Sarah Orne Jewett, 1849–1909,
Country Byways

I think that if ever a mortal heard the voice of God it would be a garden at the cool of day.

F. Frankfort Moore
(writer)

One of the most delightful things about a garden is the anticipation it provides.

W. E. Johns
(1893–1968, author)

I have a garden of my own,
Shining with flowers of every hue;
I love it dearly while alone,
But I shall love it more with you.

Thomas Moore
(1779–1852, writer)

*W*hen I was most tired, particularly after a hot safari in the dry, dusty plains, I always found relaxation and refreshment in my garden. It was my shop window of loveliness, and Nature changed it regularly that I might feast my hungry eyes upon it. Lone female that I was, this was my special world of beauty: these were my changing styles and my fashion parade.

Osa Johnson
(explorer, writer)

I perhaps owe having become a painter to flowers.

Claude Monet
(1840–1926, French painter)

A botanical garden is not only the most useful and most important of public improvements, but it also comprises within a small compass the history of the vegetable species of our own country.

Dr. Samuel Mitchell
(horticulturist)

*Y*ou must not praise the elegance of an Englishman's house—though you may always be impressed by the garden.

> *George Mikes*
> *(1912–1987, English writer)*

*J*une 10, in the afternoon, I went to Peckham, a pretty village which lies three miles from London in Surrey, where Mr. Peter Collinson has a beautiful little garden, full of all kinds of the rarest plants, especially American ones, which can endure the English climate and stand out the whole winter. However neat and small it is, there is scarcely a garden where so many kinds of trees and plants, especially the rarest, are to be found. Peter Collinson uses knucklebones for his borders and he explained to me his method of sowing mistletoe and also experiments he had made with cranberries. He thinks it is best for a garden to have morning sun so that it may help dry up the vapours. Quadrilateral is the best shape and is one which he had adopted, whereas the gardens of the Duke of Richmond are round. The sun is not so effective . . .

> *Peter Kalm, 1748 (pupil and friend of*
> *Carl Linnaeus [botanist],*
> *and link between John Bartram [botanist]*
> *and Peter Collinson)*

A Heaven on Earth: For blissful Paradise Of God the garden was, by him on the east Of Eden planted.

> *John Milton*
> *(1608–1674, English epic poet)*

*O*utside the wall of green made by tall spruces, I heard voices. One said: "Do look at those peonies— aren't they wonderful!" I called to the strangers, asking them to enter, to wander where they would. In they came, and we spent a few moments together enjoying the soft sight of many blooming flowers, the sweet scents in the dew, the rich greens of foliage and turf in the fading light; then I left them still exclaiming over the beauty of what they saw. But we had had together, these three unknown women and I, that satisfaction of the common beauty of the common things of the common life; and such moments leave one happier.

Louisa Yeomans King,
Chronicles of the Garden

*T*here seems to be considerable support for the theory that plants are good for people, and I see this every day in my work in Central Park. Even those most unsophisticated about plants; and who will never know a *Thalictrum* from a *Lamiastrum*, seem to respond to the patterns and rhythms of a garden. Graffiti have virtually disappeared, trash ends up in trash cans. Even teenagers fully untapped of energy have learned to come into the Garden and actually sit down.

Lynden B. Miller,
Perennial Plant Association Symposium,
1986 (horticulturist)

*E*very gardener's life begins with an act of seduction, whether it comes at age 10 or at age 50.

Allen Lacy (garden columnist)

The abundance of every thing around was so great, that . . . overripe fruit strewed the ground unheeded, while peas and beanstalks, still loaded, were blackening and yellowing in the sun; and vegetables running on all sides to waste.

This prodigality of wealth was, however, the only thing at all militated, to the judicious eye, against the pleasure afforded by the spectacle of these fine, well-ordered gardens.

Anne Marsh
(English writer)

An album is a garden, not for show
Planted, but use; where wholesome herbs should grow.

Charles Lamb
(1775–1834, English essayist)

I have a garden of my own,
But so with roses overgrown,
And lilies, that you would guess
To be a little wilderness.

Andrew Marvell
(1621–1678, English poet, satirist)

There is nothing more agreeable in a garden than good shade, and without it a garden is nothing.

Batty Langley,
New Principles of Gardening

As a boundary fence, especially upon the roadside, there is much to be said in favor of the hedge. Nothing gives a neighborhood such a finished rural aspect, as to have the roads bordered by hedges.

George A. Martin,
Fences, Gates and Bridges:
A Practical Manual, *1981*

Gardens faithfully reflect their creators and the civilization from which they arise.

Librairie Larousse,
Gardening and Gardens

For me it started with a house in the country and a new landscape, then learning the names of plants, buying them, too many, dividing them for friends, getting their surplus, looking at catalogues and going to nurseries, buying more plants, now old garden books, eventually finding myself in a garden too big to care for unless I quit my job. This, I think, is the general pattern of a gardener's life in its beginning stages.

Bonnie Marranca,
American Garden Writing, *1989*

Creating a garden is an exciting adventure.

Librairie Larousse,
Gardening and Gardens

*W*hoever makes a garden
Has, oh, so many friends!—
The glory of the morning,
The dew when daylight ends.

Douglas Malloch
(American poet,
syndicated writer)

*W*hile I had learned to draw, to paint and to grow
plants, it was not until I understood garden as the art
which organizes outdoor space for man's use, comfort
and pleasure that I accepted it as essential rather than
as decoration.

Carlton B. Lees,
Gardens, Plants and Man
(b. 1924, executive director,
Massachussetts Horticultural Society,
landscape designer, photographer)

*C*an we conceive what humanity would be if it did
not know the flowers?

Maurice Maeterlinck
(1862–1949, Belgian poet, dramatist)

*T*he weakness of American gardening is the petu-
nia-bed thinking of many who play a leading role in
it, and a lack of understanding of it as environment.

Carlton B. Lees,
Gardens, Plants and Man
(b. 1924, executive director,
Massachusetts Horticultural Society,
landscape designer, photographer)

A garden is a complex of aesthetic and plastic intentions; and the plant is, to a landscape artist, not only a plant—rare, unusual, ordinary or doomed to disappearance—but it is also a color, shape, a volume or an arabesque in itself.

Roberto Burle Marx
(landscape designer)

G ardens, like paintings and symphonies, are beyond words.

Carlton B. Lees,
Gardens, Plants and Man
(b. 1924, Executive Director,
Massachusetts Horticultural Society,
landscape designer, photographer)

A fter one has been a gardener for a time, the urge to collect more than plants becomes apparent, and the plantsman turns to books about gardening, books to while away the nonproductive hours far from the yard, to entertain the intellect, to bring pictures to the mind's eye.

H. Peter Loewer,
Month-By-Month Garden Almanac

P erhaps no word of six letters concentrates so much satisfaction as the word "garden."

Richard Le Gallienne,
contributor to
Corners of Grey Old Garden
(1866–1947, English poet)

One of the wonderful things about gardening is that there is no one way about it.

H. Peter Loewer,
Month-By-Month Gardem Almanac

We ought to be custodians, not owners; it should be our privilege to help the living things in our garden. A really good man should want to turn a garden, even if it is not his own; this is the decisive test.

Clare Leighton
(American writer)

I walk down the garden paths,
And all the daffodils
Are blowing, and the bright blue squills.
I walk down the patterned garden-paths
In my stiff, brocaded gown.
With my powdered hair, and jewelled fan,
I too am a rare
Pattern. As I wander down the garden paths.

Amy Lowell
(1874–1924, American poet)

Chapter 2
Toil and Reward

I hope in time to have the reputation of being as good a *farmeress* as my partner has of being a good statesman.

Abigail Adams
(1744–1818 first lady,
wife of U.S. president John Adams)

A small herb garden can be both utilitarian and aesthetic, offering culinary treats and aromatic experience.

Rhoda Specht Tarantino,
Small Gardens Are More Fun

P reserving topsoil means keeping it in place, and it means keeping this soil clean. Soil should never be treated as dirt.

Roger B. Swain,
Horticulture Magazine,
August/September, 1992 (Botanist)

H ere alone I move
Slowly in this small garden, deeply regarding
The flower, the tree, the grass, the weed, I love;
Dig here, plant there, or with a sickle cut
The too thick clover.

Conrad Aiken
(1889–1973, American writer)

47

I entertain in the garden. I keep a mental calendar of what happens, when and where so that I can set a table in the pumpkin patch when the potirons are huge and bright orange, or near the white 'Belle of Georgia' peaches so that we can pick our dessert right off the trees.

Martha Stewart,
Martha Stewart's Gardening Month by Month
(American life-style writer, magazine editor)

*I*t is not enough for a gardener to love flowers; he must also hate weeds.

Anonymous

I had always loved gardening, and therefore, I decided that though I would certainly make many mistakes, I would do the whole thing, including the landscaping, myself . . .

Harvey Ladew,
Random Recollections

A man of words and not of deeds
Is like a garden full of weeds.

Anonymous,
"A Man of Words and Not of Deeds"
(nursery rhyme)

*T*o begin with, there is no such thing as a "born" gardener. Even the most famous and accomplished gardeners had to start at the beginning, and all gardeners are perpetual students.

Pamela Jones,
How Does Your Garden Grow?
(professional gardener, landscape artist)

*S*he led me, hand in Hand, and we went into her
    garden to converse together.
There She made me taste of excellent honey.
The rushes of the garden were verdant, and all its
    bushes were flourishing.

Anonymous, from an Egyptian poem

*P*eople say British food is terrible, but it's not. It's wonderful. We set out to find the wonder. We don't want green and red peppers grown under glass in Holland and packed in plastic containers. We want the gnarled thing from our own garden.

Keith Floyd (writer)

*T*he popularity of vegetable gardening has waxed and waned, but it is usually at its peak during times of war or economic stress, so it is not surprising that there is greater enthusiasm now for a supply of home-grown vegetables.

John Brookes,
A Place in the Country
(English landscape designer)

49

Orchard of unfalling fruit,
Grape and apple, herb and root,
Of all the wealth that gardens give whereby
man can eat and live

Asmenius
(Latin poet)

I wish my mother was alive to hear me say this: I *love* vegetables, all kinds and colors of vegetables. Even vegetables that I thought I disliked only a few years ago. Now I can't think of one vegetable I wouldn't enjoy (except perhaps those I have yet to taste).

Jane Brody,
Jane Brody's Good Food Gourmet
(b. 1941, American cookbook columnist, writer)

The gardener, for his easy pains
Repaid a hundred fold, in gains
Of lighter limb and clearer sight,
Reaps a pure harvest of delight.

Asmenius
(Latin poet)

The best kind of gardening is a form of home production capable of considerable independence of outside sources.

Wendell Berry,
"The Reactor and the Garden"
(b. 1934, poet, novelist, essayist)

. . . The food was so fresh and beautiful to look at—
oranges, lemons, and grapefruit hanging from trees.
So that's how they grew. Fantastic!

Lauren Bacall,
By Myself
(b. 1924, American actress)

I always urge my students to taste things raw, and
keep tasting as they cook. If you don't understand
your materials and how they're changing, cooking is
like blundering through the subway with the lights
off. This is especially true with vegetables. I wonder
how many centuries it took for us to forget and then,
only recently, to rediscover how good most of them
are when eaten raw.

James Beard,
The New James Beard
(1903–1985, chef)

The objection to gardening is that by the time your
back gets used to it, your enthusiasm is gone.

Baltimore Sun

Go little book, and wish to all
Flowers in the garden, meat in the hall

Robert Louis Stevenson,
Underwoods,
1887 (1850–1894, English writer)

*T*he best way to get real enjoyment out of a garden is to put on a wide straw hat, dress in thin, loose-fitting clothes, hold a trowel in one hand and a cold drink in the other, and tell the man where to dig.

Charles Barr (writer)

*O*f all of the operations connected with horticulture, pruning, shaping, and training bring the person into closest contact and sympathy with his plant.

Liberty Hyde Bailey
(1858–1954, horticulturist)

*S*ince 10 years old, a great inclination to plants and know all that I once observed by sight, though not their proper names, having no person nor books to instruct me.

John Bartram
(1699–1777 botanist)

A gardener not wholly herbivorous
From wilting was out to deliver us.
With blood, sweat and toil
She composted the soil
And made even the lilies carnivorous.

Cecil Beaton
(1904–1980,
British photographer)

$\mathcal{G}$ardening needs to be approached with a generous sprinkling of good old-fashioned common sense; otherwise you'll resemble the overwrought mother who constantly has one finger on her son's pulse and a thermometer in his mouth.

Janet Chadwick, b. 1933,
How to Live on Almost Nothing
and Have Plenty

$\mathcal{T}$he person who "knows it all" is never so much at home as in someone else's flower garden, where the principal labor may be done with the tongue.

Ida D. Bennett,
The Flower Garden:
A Handbook of Practical Garden Lore

$\mathcal{M}$any people garden for the pleasure and relaxation it gives them, and consequently they are not terribly concerned about how much time the garden takes each week. For others of us, time is always in short supply. We have jobs, families to care for and enjoy, and a desire for some fun and recreation once in a while. Whether or not we even have a garden may come down to the question of the availability of our time.

Jeff Ball, 60-Minute Garden

$\mathcal{T}$he delicate flavor of a raw mushroom always takes me back to a special field on a farm we owned in Oregon. As a boy I'd get up at dawn to harvest the night's crop, if any, and bring back a pailful for breakfast when the luck was good.

James Beard, The New James Beard
(1903–1985, American chef)

53

$\mathscr{I}$ want death to find me planting my cabbages.

Michel Eyquem de Montaigne,
Essays
(1533–1592, French writer)

$\mathscr{T}$he phrase Shrinking Violet is really an overworked oxymoron. Violets have not inherited their corner of the earth due to any intrinsic meekness.

Peter Bernhardt,
Wily Violets and Underground Orchids
1989 (botanist)

$\mathscr{L}$et me work all day in my garden, the next day ramble in the fields and woods, with a little reading, and the third day I can give myself to literary pursuits with a new freshness and vigor.

John Burroughs,
The Heart of Burroughs Journals
(1837–1921, American naturalist)

$\mathscr{O}$ne of the most important local resources that a garden makes available for use is the gardener's own body. At a time when the national economy is largely based on buying and selling substitutes for common bodily energies and functions, a garden restores the body to its usefulness—a victory for our species.

Wendell Berry, b. 1934,
The Gift of Good Land:
Further Essays Cultural and Agricultural, *1981*

*T*he gardener, like the gamekeeper, is never a person who will allow you to teach him anything.

William Henry Hudson,
The Book of a Naturalist
(1841–1922, English naturalist)

*U*nseen they pour blessing,
And Joy without ceasing,
On each bud and blossom,
And each sleeping bosom.

William Blake
(1757–1827, English poet, painter)

*N*ature thrives on patience; man on impatience.

Paul Boese,
as quoted by Reader's Digest,
September 1968 (writer)

*T*here is a little hop-garden in which I used to work when from eight to ten years old; from which I have scores of times run to follow the hounds, leaving the hoe to do the best that it could to destroy the weeds.

William Cobbett
(1763–1835, writer, editor, politician)

*Y*ou fight dandelions all weekend, and late Monday afternoon there they are, pert as all get out, in full and gorgeous bloom, pretty as can be, thriving as only dandelions can in the face of adversity.

Hal Borland
(1900–1978, nature writer)

I would have showed him the garden-seat, under which Sir William Temple's heart was buried, agreeable to his will; but, the seat was gone, also the wall at the back of it; and the exquisitely beautiful little lawn in which the seat stood, was turned into a parcel of divers-shaped, cockney-clumps, planted according to the strictest rules of artificial and refined vulgarity.

William Cobbett
(1763–1835, writer, editor, politician)

*W*e went out to the garden and found everything thriving and in its own way, grateful. We picked heads of the most beautiful lettuce you ever saw, and we cut asparagus. Then we came in and washed the asparagus, steamed it, and had a feast of asparagus and lettuce not half an hour out of the garden . . .

Hal Borland, 1900–1978
Hal Borland's Book of Days

*T*hey are the most beautiful clumps of trees that I ever saw in my life. They were, indeed, planted by a clever and most trusty servant, who, to say all that can be said in his praise, is, that he is worthy of such a master as he has.

William Cobbett
(1763–1835, writer, editor, politician)

*I*f you value your time, consider carefully the extent of your vegetable garden, for what seemed initially an economic virtue can become a time-consuming vice.

John Brookes,
(English landscape designer)
A Place in the Country

$\mathcal{W}$ithout my work in the garden with hoe and cultivator, the vegetable patch would be the scene of war to death among quack grass, pig weed, purslane, and German weed. Even the vigorous asparagus needs my help to maintain anything approaching dominance in its small area.

> Hal Borland, 1900–1978,
> Hal Borland's Book of Days

(On planting shrubbery/landscaping:)

$\mathcal{O}$ne of my children called from the house, "Mommy! Daddy! The shrubbery is here!" "Where?" asked my husband. "On the dining room table with the mail." We stood around the table. No one spoke as we viewed the envelope holding five maples, eight taxus, six evergreens, two ash, four locust, 109 living rose hedge plants, two flowering mother-in-law tongues, and a grove of 15 assorted, colorful fruit trees. My son had more foliage than that growing under his bed . . .

By noon the next day we had planted the entire package. "Whatya think?" asked my husband. "I think it looks like a missile site," I grumbled.

> Erma Bombeck, "Lot No. 15436 . . . Where Are You?"
> from The Grass Is Always Greener Over the
> Septic Tank, 1985 (American humor writer)

$\mathcal{M}$an was not made to rust out in idleness. A degree of exercise is as necessary for the preservation of health, both of body and mind, as his daily food. And what exercise is more fitting, or more appropriate for one who is in the decline of life, than that of superintending a well ordered garden?

> Joseph Breck,
> New Book of Flowers

*N*ever, in the history of the world, have so many men sacrificed so much, so often, at such a price, for so little . . . There wasn't a night he wasn't hauling bags of manure and nitrogen, trimming around walks and trees on his hands and knees, watering, mulching and clipping . . . Every new week there was some new gimmick to buy that sent everyone racing to the garden center.

Erma Bombeck, "The Suburban Lawn,"
from The Grass Is Always Greener
Over the Septic Tank, *1985*
(American humor writer, columnist)

$\mathcal{M}$aking a garden is not a gentle hobby for the elderly, to be picked up and laid down like a game of solitare. It is a grand passion. It seizes a person whole, and once it has done so he will have to accept that his life is going to be radically changed.

May Sarton,
Plant Dreaming Deep, *1983*
(poet, novelist)

$\mathcal{T}$he American gardener is obsessed with planting things farther apart for maintenance. The neat and tidy bit is a North American obsession. Maintenance people don't often know about plants, they just want to get in and out.

John Brookes (English landscape designer)

$\mathcal{O}$ne of the things gardening does for me is to provide a way of resting without being bored; a day divided between writing in the morning and gardening in the afternoon has a good balance, it is possible to maintain what might be called perfect pitch, total awareness, for a good many hours of such a day. And gardening is so rich in sensuous pleasures that I hardly notice its solitariness.

May Sarton,
Plant Dreaming Deep, *1983*
(poet, novelist)

$\mathcal{W}$hen I show slides of English gardens, it's what everybody ooohs and aaahs about. We cut back and don't let it develop in a full way but rather let it be wild.

John Brookes (English landscape designer)

(On water shortage:)

I went on watering, after sunset a little at a time, hoping to revive what looked most wilted. But quick shallow watering hardly helps deep-rooted perennials and may actually do harm; it does keep annuals alive, as well as cucumbers and zucchini, the great fleshy leaves of which may droop in a pitiful way by noon but revive again if given a small drink. I felt responsible as if the garden had become a host of pleading children, and I who had given them life had fallen under a curse. To an absurd extent I was aware of the thirst all around me.

May Sarton,
Plant Dreaming Deep, *1983*
(poet, novelist)

*I*t is simply that in all life on earth as in all good agriculture there are no short-cuts that by-pass Nature and the nature of man himself and animals, trees, rocks and streams. Every attempt at a formula, a short-cut, a panacea, always ends in negation and destruction.

Louis Broomfield,
Malabar Farm

*W*eeds can be raised cheaper than most other crops, because they will bear more neglect. But they don't pay in the end. They are the little vices that beset plant life, and are to be got rid of the best way we know how.

Farmer's Almanac, *1881*

*F*or many gardeners, the real hallmark of their gardening success is not that their garden looks attractive and is admired by all-comers but that they can dine on the results of their labors.

Stefan Buczacki,
Conran's Basic Book of Home Gardening, 1988
(British garden writer, broadcaster)

*H*ere then is the terrible dilemma. The lands that are shred for needed minerals are the same lands that feed, clothe and shelter us. When we dig, we shrink our farms. There is no land to spare.

Harry M. Caudell (writer)

*O*ld-world plants and flowers linger still like heirlooms in the farmhouse garden, though their pleasant odor is oft-times checked by the gaseous fumes from the furnaces of the steam-ploughing engines as they pass along the road to their labour. Then a dark vapour rises above the tops of the green elms, and the old walls tremble and the earth itself quakes beneath the pressure of the iron giant. While the atmosphere is tainted with the smell of cotton waste and oil. How little these accord with the quiet sunny slumber of the homestead!

Richard Jeffries
(1848–1887, writer)

*N*ew dandelions in the short, new grass, through all their rapid stages daily pass.

John Albee (writer)

I am very much a fresh vegetable buff, and we use few convenience vegetables in our family simply because we think so many of them lose their flavor when canned or frozen.

Julia Child, b. 1912,
From Julia Child's Kitchen (chef)

*W*e do not feel, as Humphrey Repton, the landscape gardener, felt in his epitaph, that our dust is going to turn into roses. Dust we believe simply to be dust.

Geoffrey Grigson
(1905–1985, writer)

*T*o lift and punctuate and tear apart the soil is a labor—of pleasure—always accompanied by an exultation that no unprofitable exercise can ever provide.

Colette
(1873–1954, French novelist)

*A*nd so it criticized each flower,
This so precious seed;
Until it woke one summer hour,
And found itself a weed.

Mildred Howells,
"The Different Seed" (poet)

*T*here are cases in which the blade springs, but the plant does not go on to flower. There are cases where it flowers, but no fruit is subsequently produced.

Confucius
(551–479 B.C., Chinese philosopher)

When you open up the earth even for a mere cabbage-patch you always feel like the first man, the master, the husband with no rival. The earth you open up has no longer any past—only a future.

Colette
(1873–1954, French novelist)

The little slender flower had more courage than the green leaves, for they were but half expanded and half grown, but the blossom was spread full out. I uprooted it rashly, and I felt as if I had been committing an outrage, so I planted it again. It will have but a stormy life of it, but let it live if it can . . .

Dorothy Wordsworth
(1771–1855, writer)

But just for one's health, as you are saying, it is very necessary to work in the garden and to see the flowers growing. I myself am quite absorbed by the immeasurable plain with cornfields against the hills, immense as a delicate yellow, delicate soft green, delicate violet of a ploughed and weeded piece of soil, regularly chequered by the green of flowering potato-plants, everything under a sky with delicate blue, white, pink, violet tones. I am in a mood of nearly too great calmness to paint this.

Vincent Van Gogh,
letter from Auvers-Sur-Oise, France,
to his mother and sister in 1890 (1853–1890,
marked by his mother as
"very last letter from Auvers")
(Dutch painter)

$\mathcal{T}$he scents of plants are like unseen ghosts. They sneak upon you as you round a turn in the garden, before you can see the plants from which they came.

Barbara Damrosch,
Theme Gardens, *1982*
(American landscape designer)

$\mathcal{H}$ardy and steady, and engrossing labor with the hands, especially out of doors, is invaluable to the literary man and serves him directly. Here I have been for six days surveying the woods, and yet when I get home at evening somewhat weary at least, and beginning to feel that I have nerves, I find myself more susceptible than usual to the finest influences, as music and poetry. The very air can intoxicate me, or the least sight or sound, as if my finer senses had acquired an appetite by their fast.

Henry David Thoreau,
Autumn
(1817–1862, American philosopher, naturalist)

$\mathcal{W}$hy such a name as "foxes gloves" was bestowed upon this plant it is difficult to say, perhaps from the bare resemblance to finger-cases presented by its flower: but I am not one of those who cavil or jeer at the common, or "vulgar names," as we are in the habit of denominating the unscientific appellations of plants; for we must remember that the culling of herbs and samples, and compounding preparations from them, to relieve the sufferings of nature, were the first rudiments of all our knowledge, the most grateful exertion of human talent, and, after food and clothing, the most necessary objects of life.

John Leonard Knapp (soldier, illustrator, writer)

The more you learn about gardening and the harder you work at it, the more beautiful your garden will be.

Barbara Damrosch,
Theme Gardens, 1982
(American landscape designer)

One of the most exciting things about planning a garden is the many and varied ways there are to play with color—from blending great masses of color to highlighting the gemlike glow of a single blossom.

Barbara Damrosch,
Theme Gardens, 1982
(American landscape designer)

Contrary to the popular belief of city slickers, "dirt" is not "soil." Dirt is the stuff on your window sills, and under the rug. Soil is what plants have their roots in . . . and there's a big difference.

Linda Yang, b. 1937
The Terrace Gardener's Handbook, 1982

The truth is, I have a brown thumb. Every green thing I touch withers.

Robertson Davies (author)

Gardening should really be done in blinders. Its distractions are tempering and persistent, and only by stern exercise of will do I ever finish one job without being loved off to another.

Richardson Wright
(1908–1960, magazine editor, garden writer)

The more help a man has in his garden, the less it belongs to him.

W. H. Davies (b. 1913, writer)

There is no doubt about it, the basic satisfaction in farming is manure, that always suggests that life can be cyclic and chemically perfect and aromatic and continuous.

E. B. White
(1899–1985, American essayist, writer)

The green of the meadows, the scent of the flowers, the shade of the trees and the fragrant showers refresh me and everything in its labours.

De Berceo (English poet)

Trivial annoyances slough off in a garden and problems often solve themselves there as you weed and plant. Gardening is such satisfyingly creative work, too; you can see the beautiful results of your efforts, not like the frustration of a poor golf score.

Helen Van Pelt Wilson, b. 1901,
Helen Van Pelt Wilson's
Own Garden and Landscape Book

I must tell you that I have had a whole field of garlic planted for your benefit, so that when you come, we may be able to have plenty of your favourite dishes!

Beatrice D'Este (writer)

*F*rom a garden comes health of body and mind. You keep limber there, heaven knows, and gardening isn't like games that require club membership, and special garments and equipment; all you need is old clothes and plenty of old shoes, at least six pairs a season, easily acquired by making your new ones old as you simply forget to change.

Helen Van Pelt Wilson, b. 1901,
Helen Van Pelt Wilson's
Own Garden and Landscape Book

*E*very flower is a soul blossoming out to nature.

Gerard De Nerval
(1808–1855, writer)

*N*o matter how cleaned up I am when they come in, my friends say they always see one to three *wet* shoes at the back door, evidence of my only just-stopped activity in the garden.

Helen Van Pelt Wilson, b. 1901,
Helen Van Pelt Wilson's
Own Garden and Landscape Book

*W*e cannot eat the fruit while the tree is in blossom.

Benjamin Disraeli
(1804–1881, English statesman)

*I*n our anxiety for a frost-to-frost display of color we are apt to overlook the boom of simple green—the intrinsic beauty and value of foliage.

Louise Beebe Wilder,
Color in My Garden

*I*f Elvis Presley had eaten green vegetables he'd still be alive.

Ian Drury (writer)

*W*e know, deep down in our hearts, that . . . a tablet of fertilizer does not, by itself, produce flowers in miraculous abundance, that a single spray will not mean complete freedom from pests, that few plants fulfill all claims . . . But we are eternal gamblers; perhaps this time it will all come true.

Cynthia Westcott, 1898–1983,
Are You Your Garden's Worst Pest

(The ideal garden:)

A charming paradisiacal mingling of all that was pleasant to the eyes and good for food . . . You gathered a Moss Rose one moment and a bunch of currants the next; you were in a delicious fluctuation between the scent of Jasmine and the juice of Gooseberries; the crimson of a Carnation was carried out in the lurking of the neighboring Strawberry Beds.

George Eliot
(1819–1880, English poet)

A garden is an awful responsibility. You never know what you may be aiding to grow it.

Charles Dudley Warner
(1829–1900, American novelist, essayist)

*H*e who knows what sweet and virtues are in the ground, the waters, the plants, the heavens, and how to come at these enchantments, is the rich and royal man.

Ralph Waldo Emerson
(1803–1882, philosopher, writer)

*T*o own a bit of ground, to scratch it with a hoe, to plant seeds, and watch the renewal of life—this is the commonest delight of the race, the most satisfying thing a man can do.

Charles Dudley Warner
(1829–1900, American novelist, essayist)

*N*ature seems a dissipated hussy. She seduces us from all work; listen to her rustling leaves—to the invitations which each blue peak and rolling river and fork of woodland road offers—And we should never wield the shovel or the trowel.

Ralph Waldo Emerson
(1803–1882, philosopher, writer)

*W*hat a man needs in gardening is a cast-iron back, with a hinge in it.

Charles Dudley Warner,
My Summer in a garden
(1829–1990, American novelist, essayist)

*W*hat is a weed? A plant whose virtues have not yet been discovered.

Ralph Waldo Emerson
(1803–1882, philosopher, writer)

With holly and ivy
So green and so gay,
We deck up our houses
As fresh as the day.
With bays and rosemary,
And laurel complete:
And every one now
Is a king in conceit.

Unknown

The health of your garden is as much "the stuff of life" as the compost, fertilizer, and mulch that sustain it.

Ruth Shaw Ernst,
The Naturalist's Garden

Now o'er his corn, the sturdy farmer looks, and swells with satisfaction, to behold the plenteous harvest that repaid his toil.

Unknown

I have here only made a nosegay of culled flowers, and have brought nothing of my own but the thread that ties them together.

Michel Eyquem de Montaigne
(1533–1592, French writer)

The hardest thing to raise in my garden is my knees.

Unknown

An old lady's advice on choosing a gardener: Look at his trousers. If they're patched in the knees you want him; if they're patched in the seat, you don't.

Farmer's Journal,
Belfast

A tool is but the extension of a man's hand.

Unknown

The best I can find to say of these coarse rampageous violets is that they will thrive anywhere and make unobtrusive masses in any cool, good soil.

Reginald Farrer
(1880–1920, garden writer)

If of this plant you don't see many,
Then be a good guy and don't pick any.

Unknown

As I weed and cultivate the basils, savories, and thymes in my garden, touch their furry or glossy leaves, and breathe in their spicy scent, they seem like such old friends it is difficult to realize that only three years ago these aromatic herbs, except for the parsley, sages and mint, were quite unknown to me.

Helen Morgenthau Fox,
1885–1974,
Gardening with Herbs for
Flavor and Fragrance

As you sow, so shall you reap.

Unknown

Flowers often grow more beautifully on dung-hills than in gardens that look beautifully kept.

Saint Francis De Salery (writer)

This rule in gardening ne'er forget to sow dry and set wet.

Unknown

He that would have the fruit must climb the tree.

Thomas Fuller, M.D.
(1608–1661, English physician, writer)

Oh, treat the wild flowers gently,
And call them as they're named.
For everything that's wild dear child,
Is anxious to be tamed.

Unknown

As is the gardener, so is the garden.

Thomas Fuller, M.D.
(1608–1661, English physican, writer)

*T*raining is everything. The peach was once a bitter almond; cauliflower is nothing but cabbage with a college education.

Mark Twain
(1835–1910, American writer)

*E*ach tree should have the same cared-for appearance that a well-groomed horse presents in the satin shine of his coat.

Frances Garnet,
Gardens: Their Form and Design
(The Viscountess Wolseley)

*E*rror is a hardy plant: it flourisheth in every soil.

Martin Farquhar Tupper
(1810–1889, English moralist, writer)

*H*ow do you know that the fruit is ripe? Simply because it leaves the branch.

André Gide
(1869–1951, French novelist)

*T*he work in the vegetables—Gertrude Stein was undertaking for the moment the care of the flowers and box hedges—was a full-time job and more. Later it became a joke, Gertrude Stein asking me what I saw when I closed my eyes, and I answered, Weeds. That she said was not the answer, and so the weeds were changed to strawberries.

Alice B. Toklas,
The Alice B. Toklas Cookbook
(1877–1967 writer, companion to Gertrude Stein)

$\mathcal{D}$uring the years of my childhood . . . we planted an annual garden. It sounds blissful but the memories are not all happy ones. I detested that garden. Out in the hot sun to hoe, up at the crack of dawn to harvest . . . Now, I often think about that garden. For as much as I disliked the work, I loved the taste of those fresh vegetables. What I would give today to be able to pick a vine-ripened tomato still warm from the sun or pull a handful of baby beets no bigger than marbles.

Judy Gorman,
Judy Gorman's Vegetable Cookbook
(chef)

$\mathcal{T}$he flowers are of all heights (the stems of different lengths), and though massed, are in broken and irregular ranks, the tallest standing a little over two feet high. But there is no crushing or crowding. Each individual has room to display its full perfection. The color gathers, softly flushing from the snow white at one end, through all rose, pink, cherry, and crimson shades, to the note of darkest red; the long stems of tender green showing through the clear glass, the radiant tempered gold of each flower illuminating the whole.

Celia Thaxter,
An Island Garden, *1988*
(poet, writer)

$\mathcal{T}$he design of gardens depends on a number of factors, such as the amount of land available, the amount of man-power that is available to the owner of the garden, the prevailing taste of the time and, finally, the material available.

Richard Gover
(landscape designer)

74

. . . *I* confess that I am the sort of gardener who is forever adding plants and moving them around. My garden is destined to eventually have one of everything, though never in the same place.

Roger B. Swain,
The Practical Gardener, 1989
(biologist, TV show host)

*W*ho will the fruit that harvest yields, must take the pain.

John Grange (English poet)

*P*ractical gardening is the successful culture of plants which leaves you with time, energy and a sense of humor to spare.

Roger B. Swain,
The Practical Gardener, 1989
(biologist, TV show host)

*F*or each pure Rose
That now the Bust adorns,
The patient Gardener knows
A Hundred Thorns.

Arthur Gutterman
(American poet)

A new garden often begins with the destruction of an old one. Or what is left of one.

Roger B. Swain,
The Practical Gardener, 1989
(biologist, TV show host)

*T*hough many a rose in this garden is born
No mortal who culls one escapes from the thorn.

Hāfez
(Persian poet, philosopher)

I think I may be a better person for having given
serious time and thought and effort to gardening. I
am proud of having learned to work with nature to
encourage beauty in my backyard. The hours I have
spent cultivating the soil, weeding, planting, and just
looking at what has come to be have given me boundless pleasure. I no longer say as I once did, "I have to
work in the garden today," I say with deep contentment, "I'm gardening today." I have truly reaped the
bounty of the garden.

Martha Stewart,
Martha Stewart's
Gardening Month by Month, *1991*
(American life-style writer, magazine editor)

*W*hen thou mayest have experience pleasure from a
rose bush, If thou endurest the burden of its thorn, it
is proper.

Hāfez (Persian poet, philosopher)

*I*t is a golden maxim to cultivate the garden for the
nose, and the eyes will take care of themselves.

Robert Louis Stevenson
(1850–1894, Scottish writer)

*W*hen Wordsworth's heart with pleasure filled at a crowd of golden daffodils, it's a safe bet he didn't see them two weeks later.

Geoff Hamilton (British landscape architect)

I once saw a botanist most tenderly replace a plant he had inadvertently uprooted, though we were on a bleak hillside in Tibet, where no human being was likely to see the flower again.

Sir Francis Young Husband (writer)

... *F*or grand effect, nothing, in our estimation, can ever be produced in promiscuous planting to equal that obtained by planting in masses or in ribbon lines.

Peter Henderson, 1904–1983,
Practical Floriculture

*A*side from the junipers, there were weeds and terrible rag grass and sorrel and pampas grass. We started to dig. And we dug and we dug. Sandy with a fork, David with a fork, me with a spade. And we'd yank and pull, and together we would undermine the determined roots of the rag grass. Yank—bend—twist—pull—dig with shovel—pull with hands. Agony! My back, my hips, my fingers, my feet. Poor joints—where's the lubricant?

Katharine Hepburn,
Me
(b. 1909, American actress)

I make bean-stalks, I'm a builder, like yourself.

Edna St. Vincent Millay (poet)

A garden must be looked into, and dressed as the body.

George Herbert
(1593–1633, writer)

The gardener in his old brown hands
Turns over the brown earth,
As if he loves and understands
The flowers before their birth.

Arthur Symons
(1865–1945, English journalist, poet)

I can never lose the feeling, when I spread plant food on the lawn each spring, that somehow I am working against myself.

Burton Hillis,
as quoted in Reader's Digest, *April 1953*

When you have done your best for a flower, and it fails, you have some reason to be aggrieved.

Frank Swinnerton
(1884–1982, writer)

*O*h, tell me how my garden grows,
Now I no more may labor there;
Do still the lily and the rose
Bloom on without my fostering care?

Mildred Howells (poet)

*L*ong work it wore,
Here to account the endless progeny
Of all the weeds, that bud and blossom there;
But so much as doth need, must needs be
      counted here.

Edmund Spenser,
"The Garden of Adonis"
(1552–1599, English poet)

Th' feller who raises a garden, like th' feller who
marries for money, never figures his labor.

Frank McKinney Hubbard,
New Sayings by Abe Martin

*N*o matter how often
I level this weed,
It returns after rain
As if there is no need
To remind men who sever
Life's delicate string
That destruction is never
A permanent thing.

Mark Soifer,
as quoted by
Reader's Digest, *June 1961*

*I*n order to live off a garden, you practically have to live in it.

Frank McKinney Hubbard (writer)

*D*runk with the power of having made something grow, you become Mrs. Greenjeans—you, a person who once watered a cactus to death, you, who yanked an entire patch of baby buttercups up, mistaking the foliage for clover.

Martha Smith,
Beds I Have Known, *1990*

*P*lants are very familiar. They tend to be taken for granted and regarded with placid affection rather than with the fascination and interest they deserve.

Anthony Huxley,
Green Inheritance *(botanist)*

I have known the agony of broken fingernails and cracked shins. I have gone through two pairs of expensive waterproof Wellington boots and worn out the knees on more pairs of pants than I care to recall, consigning them to an ever-increasing stack of "gardening clothes" that now exceeds my real wardrobe.

Martha Smith,
Beds I Have Known, *1990*

*T*hose who labor in the earth are the chosen people of God, if He ever had a chosen people, whose breasts He has made His peculiar deposit for substantial and genuine virtue.

Thomas Jefferson
(1743–1826, American president)

I have known that panic of Planter's Paralysis, that wretched realization that, when you sit down after a day spent using muscles in places left unmentioned in *Gray's Anatomy*, you will never, ever rise again.

Martha Smith,
Beds I Have Known, *1990*

*M*y theory is that the flowers, appreciating how hard I try, cannot bear to disappoint me and, therefore, bloom their hearts out in recognition of this devotion.

Martha Smith,
Beds I Have Known, *1990*

*E*arth is here so kind, that just tickle her with a hoe and she laughs with a harvest.

Douglas Jerrold
(1803–1857, writer)

*N*ot useless are ye flowers; though made for pleasure,
Blooming o'er fields, and wave by day and night
From every source your sanction bids me treasure
Harmless delight.

Horace Smith
(1808–1893, English poet, parodist)

*O*ne of the many rewards of gardening is bringing the color and fragrance of flowers indoors.

Mary K. Taylor,
"How to Make Your Cut Flowers Look Fresher Longer,"
from House & Garden magazine, *July 1991*
(floral designer)

*Y*ou'll have to find the insect pests in your garden before you can identify them.

Rodale's Chemical Free Yard
and Garden, *1991*

*W*e learn from our gardens to deal with the most urgent question of time: How much is enough? We don't soup our gardens up with chemicals because our goal is *enough,* and we know that *enough* requires a modest, moderate, conserving technology.

Wendell Berry,
"The Reactor and the Garden"
(b. 1934, poet, writer)

*N*o hand is yet stretched forth to cull the fruit.

Kasmuneh (poet)

*N*ow 'tis the spring, and weeds are shallow rooted; Suffer them now and they'll o'ergrow the garden.

William Shakespeare,
Henry VI
(1564–1616, English dramatist, poet)

𝒢ardens are not made by singing "Oh, how beautiful," and sitting in the shade.

Rudyard Kipling
(1865–1936, English poet, writer)

𝒯here is no ancient gentleman but gardeners, ditchers, and grave-makers; They hold up Adam's profession.

William Shakespeare,
Hamlet
(1564–1616, English dramatist, poet)

𝒪h, Adam was a gardener, and God who made
    him sees
That half a proper gardener's work is done upon
    his knees.

Rudyard Kipling
(1865–1936, English poet, writer)

... 𝒮eek your job with thankfulness and
work till further orders,
If it's only netting strawberries or
killing slugs on borders;
And when your back stops aching and
your hands begin to harden,
You will find yourself a partner in the
Glory of the Garden.

Rudyard Kipling,
"Glory of the Garden"
(1865–1936, English poet, writer)

*S*uperfluous branches
We lop away, that bearing boughs may live.

William Shakespeare
(1564–1616, English dramatist, poet)

*S*weet flowers are slow and weeds make haste.

William Shakespeare
(1564–1616, English dramatist, poet)

*E*very man reaps what he sows—except the amateur gardener.

Cholly Knickerbocker,
as quoted in Reader's Digest,
September 1960

*F*ie on't! Oh fie! 'tis an unweeded garden,
that grows to seed; things rank and gross
in nature.

William Shakespeare
(1564–1616, English dramatist, poet)

*N*o garden is ever made once and for all, and every garden eventually reaches such a point of crisis that it must be rethought and replanted.

Allen Lacy
(American garden writer)

*T*is this provides the body healthful foods,
And gives the tiller oft its varied yield—
Delicious greens and many kinds of herbs,
The sheen of grapes and fruitage rich of trees.

Aulus Septimius Serenus
(poet)

(Written in 1991:)

I had originally calculated that getting the roots out
of the beds would take a week. A revised estimate
pushed the date of completion to late in 1999.

Allen Lacy
(American garden writer)

A garden charms, allures, gives shelter, food,
And from sad hearts removes the weight of grief
Gives strength to limbs, and captivates the eye,
Rewards man's toil with fuller recompense,
And yields the workman joy in countless forms.

Aulus Septimius Serenus
(poet)

*T*here are also a lot of trees and shrubs, planted over
the years. Sourwoods, ultexes, hollies, cotoneasters,
hybrid witch, hazels, jujobes—these and many other
woody plants have grown to have some age on them.
I can now sit in the shade that I helped to create.

Allen Lacy
(American garden writer)

$\mathcal{L}$andscaping is the first and hardest job in gardening.

Stanley Schuler
(b. 1915, garden writer)

$\mathcal{H}$abits die hard. Accustomed to thinking of the garden as a place in the sun, I did not notice the roots of all the woody plants that had invaded the flower borders, robbing them of nutrients and moisture.

Allen Lacy
(American garden writer)

$\mathcal{K}$eeping a garden neat as a pin sometimes has unhappy results.

Stanley Schuler
(b. 1915, garden writer)

*T*he act of putting into your mouth what the earth has grown is perhaps your most direct interaction with the earth.

Frances Moore Lappe, b. 1944,
Diet for a Small Planet, 1976
(ecologist, activist, author)

*A*ny garden demands as much of its maker as he has to give. But I do not need to tell you, if you are a gardener, that no other undertaking will give as great a return for the amount of effort put into it.

Elizabeth Lawrence, 1904–1985,
Gardening for Love

*B*ut nothing could exceed the freshness and beauty of the flowers, still leaded as they were with the moisture of the night, and this mysterious and shadowy hour of dawn, when they open, as if to display those treasures of purity, and shed those sweetest perfumes, which the earliest and purest of the sun's rays are alone worth to behold and possess for an instant.

George Sand, 1804–1876,
Consuelo

*T*he fairest thing in nature, a flower, still has its roots in earth and manure.

D. H. Lawrence
(1885–1930, English novelist, poet)

$\mathcal{G}$ardening is largely a question of mixing one sort of plant with another sort of plant and seeing if they marry happily together.

Vita Sackville-West
(1892–1962, British garden author, poet)

$\mathcal{I}$ have grown wise, after many years of gardening, and no longer order recklessly from wildly alluring descriptions which make every annual sound easy to grow and as brilliant as a film star. I now know that gardening is not like that.

Vita Sackville-West
(1892–1962, British garden author, poet)

$\mathcal{I}$ used to try a hundred or so new things each year, but as I grow older the days seem to get shorter—also the garden gets fuller.

Elizabeth Lawrence,
1904–1985,
Through the Garden Gate

$\mathcal{A}$nd all these [flowers] by the skill of your gardener, so comely and orderly pleased in your borders and squares, and so intermingled, that one looking thereon, cannot but wonder to see, what nature, corrected by art, can do.

William Lawson,
A New Orchard and Garden

*A*vocado growers denied publicly and indignantly the insidious, slanderous rumors that avocados were an aphrodisiac.

Waverly Root
(1903–1982, writer)

*T*o waste, to destroy, our natural resources, to skin and exhaust the land instead of using it so as to increase its usefulness, will result in undermining the days of our children the very property which we ought by right to hand down to them amplified and developed.

Theodore Roosevelt
(1858–1919, American president)

*B*ut, Kate, you're dealing in fundamentals here, fool and trick life. Watering, for instance—you must do it thoroughly. Don't be fooled by the ground being wet on top. That's no good at all . . . Don't drown the plant—just give it a chance to absorb all it can. Roots are like us—they can't be forced—they must be made to work for their own future. But steadily . . . carefully . . . given a proper environment.

David Lean, as quoted by Katharine Hepburn in Me,
1991 (English film director)

*S*ometimes it is extremely good for you to forget that there is anything in the world which needs to be done, and to do some particular thing that you want to do. Every human being needs a certain amount of time in which he can be peaceful.

Eleanor Roosevelt
(1884–1962, American humanitarian,
and wife of President Franklin D. Roosevelt)

The smell of manure, of sun on foliage, of evaporating water rose to my head; two steps farther, and I could look down into the vegetable garden enclosed within its tall pale of reeds—rich chocolate earth studded emerald green, frothed with the white of cauliflowers, jewelled with the purple globes of eggplant and the scarlet wealth of tomatoes.

Doris Lessing, b. 1919,
The Habit of Loving

(On plant selection:)

Throw away the weedy kinds. There is no lack of the best. It is easy to agree, but less easy to define either the weeds or the best.

William Robinson
(1838–1935, American writer)

To a gardener there is nothing more exasperating than a hose that just isn't long enough.

Cecil Roberts
(1892–1976, writer)

There seems to be an inherent desire in all human beings, but particularly in plant people, to know the correct name of everything.

H. Peter Loewer,
Evergreens
(garden author, illustrator)

*N*ature does not proceed by leaps and bounds.

> *Carl Linnaeus*
> *(1707–1778, Swedish botanist)*

I offer two rules for diggers: not too much, and not when wet.

> *Lee Reich (columnist)*

*L*abeling does not seem important when stacked up against tilling, plowing, digging, planting, weeding, and all the other hard work of gardening, but it is a valuable activity nonetheless.

> *H. Peter Loewer,*
> Evergreens
> *(garden author, illustrator)*

I haven't nuked this piece of earth with herbicides, as many books advise. I have simply dug out the weeds that were there and let the ground rest for a couple of weeks. I know there will be plenty of weeds, but hey, this is a wild garden.

> *Anne Raver*
> *(garden columnist)*

A weed is no more than a flower in disguise, which is seen through at once, if love give a man eyes.

> *James Russell Lowell*
> *(1819–1891, American poet)*

*L*et not your garden want one blooming fair,
Or grateful scent; last sparing of your pains,
you leave expos'd to shame the naked scenes:
Nor can your labor fall, if you but know
The proper mould, and season when to sow.

Rene Rapin
(French Jesuit, poet)

*F*or thee the wonder-working earth puts forth sweet
flowers.

Lucretius (96–55 B.C., Roman poet)

*A*ll gardeners know better than other gardeners.

Chinese proverb

*F*ound a little patch up in the village of Bulson . . .
Proprietor had nothing but potatoes; but what a feast
he laid before me. Served them in five different
courses—potato soup, potato fricassee, potatoes
creamed, potato salad and finished with potato. It
may be because I had not eaten for 36 hours, but that
meal seems the best I ever had.

Douglas MacArthur
(1880–1964, American military general)

*T*he legume family is so talented, that if its members
were humans, they would be the Leakeys, the Buck-
leys, or perhaps the Osmonds.

Jonathan Probber
(American humorist)

And at noon he would come
Up from the garden, his hard crooked hands
Gentle with earth, his knees earth-stained, smelling
Of sun, of summer, the old gardener, like
A priest, like an interpreter, and bend
Over his baskets.

Archibald MacLeish
(1892–1982, American poet)

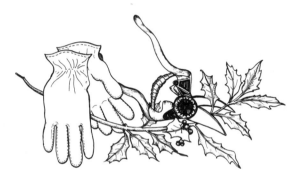

It was not until my children were growing up that I really found time again to enjoy flowers and come to know those of my new country. For to have complete satisfaction from flowers you must have time to spend with them. There must be rapport. I talk to them and they talk to me.

Princess Grace of Monaco, 1929–1982,
My Book of Flowers *(Grace Kelly)*

To get the best results you must talk to your vegetables.

Prince Charles
(b. 1948, H.R.H. Prince of Wales)

93

The cherry tomato is a marvelous invention, producing as it does a satisfactorily explosive squish when bitten.

Miss Manners
(American columnist)

. . . Roses are the only flowers at garden-parties; the only flowers that everybody is certain of knowing.

Katherine Mansfield,
"The Garden Party"
(1888–1923, writer)

(A passionate response when asked by his students about how to tell when your plants need water:)

Don't be afraid to ruin your manicure—stick your fingers into the soil and find out how wet it is!

Louis Politi
(horticulturist, New York Botanical Gardens)

What wonderous life is this I lead?
Ripe apples drop about my head;
The luscious clusters of the vine
Upon my mouth do crush their wine;
The nectarine and curious peach
Into my hands themselves do reach.

Andrew Marvell
(1621–1678, English poet, satirist)

What is a weed? I have heard it said that there are sixty definitions. For me, a weed is a plant out of place.

Donald Culross Peattie (botanist)

*W*henever I write about gardening, I am struck by the amount of physical labor I seem to be describing. On paper is sounds overwhelming—but that is the nature of written directions. The reality is not so onerous.

Eleanor Perenyi,
Green Thoughts: A Writer in the Garden, *1983*

*M*en can't be trusted with pruning shears any more than they can be trusted with the grocery money in a delicatessen . . . They are like boys with new pocket knives who will not stop whittling.

Phyllis McGinley
(American essayist, writer)

*T*he more I hear of Horticulture, the more I like plain gardening.

Julian R. Meade,
Bouquets & Bitters

*O*ur family hasn't tried to set any gardening records. We don't look for cabbages as big as beach balls or zucchini as hefty as shillelaghs, we just want enough harvest to feed us. Let other gardeners seek immortality in the *Guinness Book of World Records.*

Ruth Page,
Ruth Page's Gardening Journal, *1989*
(radio show host)

*W*hat I say is that, if a fellow really likes potatoes, he must be a pretty decent sort of fellow.

A. A. Milne, 1882–1956,
(English writer)

$\mathcal{C}$ity gardeners must be a determined group. In order to make a community garden out of a vacant or abandoned lot, they must tackle bureaucracy, red tape, rubble, and garbage before beginning to plant.

Lynden B. Miller,
Perennial Plant Association Symposium, 1986
(horticulturist)

$\mathcal{C}$omposting plant leftovers not only helps feed tomorrow's new plants but fits the "waste not, want not" outlook of many of us who garden.

Ruth Page,
Ruth Page's Gardening Journal, *1989*
(radio show host)

$\mathcal{S}$o, though others are surprised to hear it on your tongue—you're a gardener. Why not praise your favorite dung?

Ruth Page,
Ruth Page's Gardening Journal, *1989*
(radio show host)

$\mathcal{T}$here are certain people
Whom certain herbs
The good digestion of disturbs.
Henry VIII
Divorced Catherine of Aragon
Because of her reckless
Use of Tarragon.

Ogden Nash
(1902–1971, American humorist)

The garden cost Amelia no end of work and worry; she tended the delicate tomato vines as though they were new born infants and suffered momentary sinking of the heart whenever she detected signs of weakness in any of the hardier vegetables. She was grateful for the till in which she could dwell as a sort of refuge from deeper thought.

Martha Ostenso,
Wild Geese

I suffer for my plants.
Victor Nelson
(garden writer)

It is not the business of the botanist to eradicate the weeds. Enough for him if he can just tell us how fast they grow.

C. Northcote Parkinson
(b. 1909, American historian, writer)

The mastery of nature is vainly believed to be an adequate substitute for self mastery.

Reinhold Niebuhr
(1892–1971, American theologian)

Chapter 3
Garden Life

[*At*] the Court of St. James* . . . I seldom meet with characters so inoffensive as my hens and chickings, or minds so well improved as my garden . . .

> *Abigail Adams*
> *(1744–1818, first lady,*
> *wife of American president John Adams)*
> *(*Reference to James Madison,*
> *U.S. president 1809–1817)*

*W*henever you mention bug and pest control to the dedicated gardener, the look that comes over his or her face gives you visions of the gardener going out to the garden with a shotgun to shoot potato bugs.

> *Janet Chadwick, b. 1933,*
> How to Live on Almost Nothing
> and Have Plenty

I value my garden more for being full of blackbirds than of cherries, and very frankly give them fruit for their songs.

> *Joseph Addison*
> *(1672–1719, English essayist, poet)*

*O*nce upon a sunny morning a man who sat in a breakfast nook looked up from his scrambled eggs to see a white unicorn with a golden horn quietly cropping the roses in the garden. The man went up to the bedroom where his wife was still asleep and woke her. "There's a unicorn in the garden," he said. "Eating roses." She opened one unfriendly eye and looked at him. "The unicorn is a mythical beast," she said, and turned her back on him. The man walked slowly downstairs and into the garden.

James Thurber, "The Unicorn in the Garden"
(1894–1961, writer)

*M*any thousands and thousands of perils and dangers beset man. He is not fully sure of his health or his life for one moment . . . but the Creator of nature who has placed us amid such dangers has mercifully provided us with a remedy—that is with all kinds of herbs, animals, and other created things to which he has given power and might.

Anonymous, fifteenth-century German

*H*ere at my feet what wonders pass,
What endless, active life is here!
What blowing daisies, fragrant grass!

Matthew Arnold
(1822–1888, English poet, essayist)

*O*ne of the most overlooked controls for insect pests is the songbird. This delightful creature is an insect-controlling machine.

Jeff Ball,
60-Minute Garden

$\mathcal{T}$here is nothing in the gardener's world that is more discouraging and frustrating than to come out one morning and find that the whole crop of beans or cabbage has been seriously damaged by insects or rabbits or some other dastardly pest that has invaded the sanctity of the vegetable patch.

Jeff Ball,
60-Minute Garden

$\mathcal{D}$ost thou not see the little plants, the little birds, the ants, the spiders, the bees working together to put in order their several parts of the universe?

Marcus Aurelius
(second-century Roman emperor, philosopher)

$\mathcal{A}$ mild morning, the windows open at breakfast, the redbreasts singing in the garden.

Dorothy Wordsworth
(1771–1855, writer)

$\mathcal{T}$he toad, without which no garden would be complete.

Charles Dudley Warner, 1893–1978,
My Summer in a Garden

$\mathcal{L}$ast summer we stretched an electrically charged wire, the sort that is used to keep cows in a pasture, along the top of the fence. Were our raiders dismayed? I'll say not. In fact, I think they enjoyed being tickled.

Roy Barrette,
The Countryman's Bed Book

$\mathcal{T}$he particular pest that afflicts one depends to a large degree upon where one gardens. The penthouse gardener is unlikely to suffer from the depredations of deer or porcupines, but cats, coming suddenly upon soft soil in which to establish sanitary facilities, will go out of their minds with joy. And English sparrows and starlings, no particular problem in the country, look upon green sprouts on a rooftop as the Israelites beheld manna falling from heaven.

Roy Barrette,
The Countryman's Bed Book

$\mathcal{F}$our pests that can do more damage to a garden in a single night than all the cutworms, aphids and caterpillars, and bean and potato beetles in existence are deer, woodchucks, porcupines, and raccoons. (Of course, there are also rabbits, cats, dogs, and small children, not to mention the cyclones, windstorms, rain, hail, frost, drought, and other Acts of God that are visited upon us for our manifold sins and wickedness.)

Roy Barrette,
The Countryman's Bed Book

$\mathcal{T}$hese birds seem of a pugnacious disposition; for they sing with an erected crest and attitudes of revelry and defiance; are shy and wild in breeding-time, avoiding neighborhoods, and haunting lonely lanes and commons; nay even the very tops of the Sussex downs, where there are bushes and covert; but in July and August they bring their broods into gardens and orchards, and make great havoc among the summer-fruits.

Gilbert White
(1720–1793, writer)

The rattle and hurry of the journey so perfectly roused it that, when I turned it [the tortoise] out on a border, it walked twice down to the bottom of my garden; however, in the evening, the weather being cold, it buried itself in a loose mould, and continues still concealed.

Gilbert White
(1720–1793, writer)

He [the tortoise] then walks on tiptoe, and is stirring by five in the morning; and, traversing the garden, examines every wicket and interstile in the fences, through which he will escape if possible: and often has eluded the care of the gardener, and wandered to some distant field.

Gilbert White
(1720–1793, writer)

I have taken to gardening a little, not a very inspiring business, though the strange debris of life which one turns up interest me.

A. C. Benson
(1862–1925, English educator, poet)

The gardener desiring perfect, unblemished fruit and ornamental plants has a pitched battle! He can win only if he is clever and well informed. May beetle and flea beetle, foliage-feeding insects, visit the plant only to feed. The young develop safely in the soil, often at some distance from the host plant. DDT, or some other poison applied to leaves, will kill these unwelcome guests.

Better Homes & Gardens
New Garden Book, *rev. ed. 1966*

*I*n the garden of the Black-Bear Inn in the town of Reading is a stream or canal running under the stables and out into the fields on the other side of the road: in this water are many carps, which lie rolling about in sight, being fed by travelers who amuse themselves by tossing them bread; but as soon as the weather grows at all severe these fishes are no longer seen, because they retire under the stables, where they remain until the return of spring. Do they lie in a torpid state? If they do not, how are they supported?

Gilbert White
(1720–1793, writer)

*O*h rose, thou art sick
The invisible worm
That flies in the night
In the howling storm

Has found out thy bed
of crimson joy,
And his dark secret love
Does thy life destroy.

William Blake
(1757–1827, English poet)

*F*or me, part of the allure of vegetable gardening is the illusion of control. I plant, I plant and I harvest. If only the rest of life was so predictable and sane! But as any gardener knows, a world that contains woodchucks, white tail deer and summer thunderstorms will always challenge our illusions.

Phyllis Rosenblum,
Albany Times Union
(garden columnist)

$\mathscr{B}$lack-caps mostly haunt orchards and gardens; while they warble their throats are wonderfully distended.

Gilbert White
(1720–1793, writer)

$\mathscr{Y}$ou can't be suspicious of a tree, or accuse a bird or a squirrel of subversion or challenge the ideology of a violet.

Hal Borland
(1960–1978, American nature writer)

$\mathscr{W}$hen brechen buds begin to swell,
And woods the blue-bird's warble know,
The yellow violet's modest bell
Peeps from the last year's leaves below.

William Cullen Bryant
(1794–1878, American poet)

These little creatures [ants] will raise a large tower of earth as thick as a man's arms in the form of a sugar loaf to a foot or a foot and a half high in the grain and long grass for in such places they cannot meet the sun on the ground so they raise these towers on the top of which they lay their eggs and as the grass or grain keeps growing they keep raising their towers till I have met with them as tall as one's knee.

John Clare
(1793–1864, poet)

A planting that butterflies would love might not be the kind of garden that a garden club would endorse.

Dave Winter (nature writer, physician)

The swallows are clothed in the golden palms where the bees are singing a busy welcome to spring they seem uncommonly fond of these flowers and gather round them in swarms

John Clare
(1793–1864, poet)

Because half a dozen grasshoppers under a fern make the field ring with their importunate chink, whilst thousands of great cattle, respond beneath the shadow of the British oak, chew the cud and are silent, pray do not imagine that those who make the noise are the only inhabitants of the field; that of course, they are many in number, or that, after all, they are other than the little shrivelled, meager, hopping though loud and troublesome insects of the hour.

Edmund Burke
(1729–1797, English statesman)

*A*fter her death the gardener does not become a butterfly, intoxicated by the perfumes of the flowers, but a garden worm tasting all the dark citrogenous, and spicy delights of the soil.

Karel Čapek
(1890–1938, writer)

*T*he robin seems to be fond of the company and haunts of men it builds its nest close to his cottage in the hovel or outhouse thatch or behind the woodbine or sweetbriar in the garden wall nor does it seem to make any secret of its dwelling where its only enemy is the cat to whom its confidence of safety often falls a prey.

John Clare
(1793–1864, poet)

*T*he world acquired a new interest when birds appeared, for the presence of birds at any time is magical in effect. They are magicians that transform every scene, make of every desert a garden of delights.

Charles C. Abbot, Days out of Doors
(1757–1829, medical doctor, American naturalist)

*I*t will soon be clear that until it has been tamed, a hose is an extraordinarily evasive and dangerous beast, for it contorts itself . . . jumps . . . wriggles . . . makes puddles of water, and dives with delight into the mess it has made.

Karel Čapek,1890–1938,
The Gardener's Year

*T*he greatest of all sources of pleasure is *discovery*. Given a plot of earth, whether in a suburban garden, a prairie, or a rain forest, it will be . . . crowded with insects.

Howard Signal Evans,
The Pleasures of Etomology
(American etomologist)

*D*istracted by the flowers
amazed at the moon
the butterfly.

Haiku by Chora
(Oriental poet)

*Y*our garden may appear to be a quiet place, but in reality it is an arena where hundreds of life-and-death dramas are played out every day. Birth and death, killing and nurturing, even intrigue and cunning are all part of the complex community of life waiting to be discovered—and sometimes struggled with in your garden.

Rosalind Creasy,
Cooking from the Garden
(cookbook writer)

. . . *W*eedkillers are even more potent than I had thought them. As a bird-lover I had always hated them on account of their destructiveness to the small birds of the homestead, the black-bird and song thrush . . .

William Henry Hudson,
The Book of a Naturalist
(1841–1922, English naturalist)

*N*ow I look down over the garden, past the gangling locust trees, past the leafy borders of the river and over the calm water to the shore and hills beyond, already facing into the cool gray of evening . . . The quiet becomes more intense. Crickets chirp faintly, then a frog down in the creek strums tentative chords and day passes into night.

Harlan Hubbard,
Payne Hollow
(painter, musician, writer)

*T*he most apparent difference between animals and vegetables is, that animals have the powers of sound, and are locomoting whereas vegetables are not able to shift themselves from the places where nature has planted them . . .

William Bartram,
The Travels of William Bartram
(1739–1823, American naturalist)

*O*n looking back, it appears that the farmhouse, garden, orchard, and rickyard at Wick are constantly visited by about thirty-five wild creatures, and, in addition, five others come now and then, making a total of forty. Of these forty, twenty-six are birds, two bats, eight quadrupeds, and four reptiles. This does not include some few additional birds that come at long intervals, nor those that simply fly overhead or are heard singing at a distance.

Richard Jeffries
(1848–1887, writer)

*I*t's a jungle out there in the insect world . . .

Robert M. Coughlin,
The Gardener's Companion

*B*e careful how you pick up a ripe apple, all glowing orange, from the grass in the orchard; roll it over with your foot first, or may chance to find that you have got a handful of wasps.

Richard Jeffries (writer)

*M*ost gardeners appreciate the good work birds do in keeping insect pests in check.

Robert M. Coughlin,
The Gardener's Companion

*W*asps are incurable drunkards. If they find something sweet and tempting they stick to it, and swill till they fall senseless to the ground.

Richard Jeffries (writer)

*I*n one spot on the hedge of the ha-ha is a row of bee-hives; the garden wall and a shrubbery shelter shade them here from the north and east, and the drop of the ha-ha gives them a clear exit and entrance. This is thought a great advantage—not to have any hedge or bush in front of the hives—because the bees, heavily laden with honey or pollen, encounter no obstruction in coming home.

Richard Jeffries (writer)

The robin is called the harbinger of spring because he makes so much noise.

Will Cuppy
(1884–1949, writer)

In spring, birds are born and they sing—have you not heard them? Their songs are pure, simple and moving in the woods!

Gerard De Nerval
(1808–1855, French writer)

Finches feeding on garden thistles are, I suppose, a common enough sight this time of year [autumn], but it underscored the matrix of functions that each organism, plant and animal, performs in nature. Who can say what the *main* function of any form of life is, what it is good for, or meant for, beyond perpetuating itself? We should not blame ourselves for using the earth's resources that is not only human nature, but the nature of all things.

Robert Finch,
Common Ground *(naturalist)*

A certain swallow built for two years together on the handles of the garden-shears, that were stuck up against the boards in an out-house, and therefore must have her nest spoiled whenever that implement was wanted.

Gilbert White
(1720–1793, writer)

111

*I*f my garden had only made me acquainted with the muck-worm, the bugs, the grasses, and the swamp of plenty in August, I should willingly pay a free tuition, but every process is lucrative to me far beyond its economy.

Ralph Waldo Emerson, Society & Solitude
(1803–1882, American philosopher)

*W*hy make so much of fragmentary blue
Or flower, or wearingstone, or open eye,
When heaven presents in sheets the solid hue?

Robert Frost
(1874–1963, American poet)

*T*o these numerous and most destructive foes all our gardens are exposed. No plant and no part of a plant is exempt from their attacks. One devours its tender leaf as it issues from the ground; another preys upon the root, and the plant perishes; another burrows into the stem, boring it in every direction until it is broken off by the wind.

William N. White,
Gardening for the South

*T*hrice welcome, darling of the spring!
Even yet thou art to me
No bird, but an invisible thing,
A voice, a mystery.

William Wordsworth
(1770–1850, English poet)

In winter, the male cardinal will not permit the female on a feeder with him. Then suddenly, in early March, they appear together, heralding the rites of spring. And when, a few weeks later, he places a seed in her bill, the wildflowers are not far away.

Jean George
(b. 1919, American writer)

Immunized early against the chemical quick fix, when I came into a garden and an appreciable pest population of my own a few years back, I declared this small, urbane patch of green a pesticide-free zone—a safe haven to birds, butterflies, fireflies, drag-onflies, worms, not to mention aphids, leafhoppers, mites, scale, mealybugs.

One season of natural free-for-all took me from organic pacifism to biological war.

Patti Hagan,
The Wall Street Journal, *June 11, 1986*
(journalist)

Any insect particularly injurious must be watched, as to its habits, mode of feeding, and its transforma-tions, in order to discover where it may be most suc-cessfully attacked.

William N. White,
Gardening for the South

How exciting is the gradual arrival of the birds in their summer plumage! To watch is like sitting at the window on Easter Sunday to observe the new bonnets.

Thomas Wentworth Higginson
(1823–1911, American essayist)

*H*ow doth the little busy bee/Improve
each shining hour,
And gather honey all the day
From every opening flower!

Isaac Watts
(1674–1748, English hymn writer)

*P*lants are continuously active, by day conjuring the
food they need out of the sunlight, water, and gases
around them, like magicians pulling rabbits out of a
hat; by night and day, using the stored energy for
growth and life.

Anthony Huxley,
Green Inheritance *(botanist)*

*M*ake no mistake about it, the chances of your
never finding any pests in your garden are nil. Most
of them are insects. Broadly speaking, these are
divided into the good guys and the bad guys. It works
something like this: While the bad guys are frolicking
about on your plants, mutilating them and breeding
merrily, the more decorous good guys quietly lick
their chops and move in. Blessed with insatiable
appetites, they proceed to dine splendidly on choice
bad guy meat, until none is left.

Pamela Jones,
How Does Your Garden Grow?
(professional gardener, landscape designer)

*T*he simplest method of all is to pick the pest and
squash it . . .

William H. Jordan, Jr.,
What's Eating Your Houseplants?

*S*ave only wizened apple trees,
whose windfalls only wasp and ant found sweet,
this garden offered nothing one could eat.

Sylvia Townsend Warner
(1893–1978, English novelist)

*S*truggling like all living things to remain alive and
to beget new life, flowers please man only incidentally
and by accident.

Josephine Von Miklos, 1900–1972,
and Evelyn Fiore,
The History, the Beauty, the Riches
of the Gardener's World

*T*he striped bug has come, the saddest of the year.
He is a moral double-ender, ironclad at that. He is
unpleasant in two ways. He burrows into the ground
so you cannot find him, and he flies away so you cannot catch him. He is rather handsome, as bugs go, but
utterly dastardly, in that he gnaws the stem of the
plant close to the ground, and ruins it without any
apparent advantage to himself.

Charles Dudley Warner,
My Summer in a Garden
(1829–1900, American novelist, essayist)

*T*he best way to tell the vegetables from the weeds is
to watch your neighbor's chickens.

Jack Judge
(English actor, songwriter)

$\mathcal{W}$e have descended into the garden and caught 300 slugs. How I love the mixture of the beautiful and the squalid in gardening. It makes it so lifelike.

Evelyn Underhill
(1875–1941, writer)

$\mathcal{N}$ow birds and trees perform their books of wonder, passersby hear wondrous news and are less sad.

Louise Labe
(French poet, linguist, feminist)

*S*teal out sometimes after sunset and walk up and down between the home end of the garden and the wild end and listen to the sounds at each.

Richard Le Gallienne
(1866–1947, English poet)

*E*vidence now supports the vision of the poet and the philosopher that plants are living, breathing, communicating creatures, endowed with personality and the attributes of soul. It is only we, in our blindness, who have insisted on considering them automata.

Peter Tomkins and Christopher Bird,
The Secret Life of Plants

*A*t no time of the year does the fellowship of the birds afford me keener enjoyment than in the dead of winter. In June one may see them everywhere . . . but in January the sight of a single brown creeper is sufficient, to brighten the day, and the twittering of a half a dozen goldfinches is like the music of angels.

Bradford Torrey
(American naturalist, orinthologist, writer)

*T*he hardest part of dealing with insect pests is often trying to figure out exactly which pest is chomping away in your garden—especially when the eating is being done when you aren't there.

Joanna Poncavage,
Organic Gardening Magazine,
July/August, 1992 (garden writer)

$\mathcal{I}$t is well known that slugs love to party; just leave a beer bottle in the garden overnight if you want proof. Set it on its side near the infant lettuce, with a tablespoon or so of beer left in it (any more would be a waste of B-vitamin complex). You are sure to find a half a dozen crocked and reeling gastropods whooping it up in the morning.

Ann Lovejoy, The Year in Bloom

$\mathcal{N}$ature will bear the closest inspection. She invites us to lay our eye level with her smallest leaf, and take an insect view of it plain.

Henry David Thoreau
(1817–1862, American naturalist, poet, essayist)

$\mathcal{I}$n order to see the birds it is necessary to become a part of the silence. One has to sit still like a mystic and wait. One soon learns that fussing, instead of achieving things, merely prevents things from happening.

Robert Lynd
(1879–1949, Anglo-Irish essayist, journalist)

$\mathcal{A}$nts are so much like human beings as to be an embarrassment. They farm fungi, raise aphids as livestock, launch armies into war, use chemical sprays to alarm and confuse enemies, capture slaves, engage in child labor, exchange information ceaselessly. They do everything but watch television.

Lewis Thomas
(b. 1913, American pathologist)

*T*here is nothing in which the birds differ more from man than the way in which they can build and yet leave a landscape as it was before.

Robert Lynd
(1879–1949, Anglo-Irish essayist, journalist)

*B*efore I knew what to do to save my garden from slugs, I have stood at evening rejoicing over rows of fresh emerald leaves just springing in rich lines along the beds, and woke in the morning to find the whole space stripped of any sign of green, as blank as a board over which a carpenter's plane has passed.

Celia Thaxter,
An Island Garden
(poet, writer)

*I*t is astonishing how violently a big branch shakes when a silly little bird has left it. I expect the bird knows it and feels immensely arrogant.

Katherine Mansfield
(1888–1923, author)

*Y*e living lamps, by whose dear light
The nightingale does sit so late,
And studying all the summer night,
Her matchless songs does meditate.

Andrew Marvell
(1621–1678, English poet, satirist)

*F*ortunately for man, the insect world is divided against itself. It is a realm of endless struggle, of fierce and deadly competition . . . It is estimated that far more than half the insects prey upon other insects.

Edwin Way Teale,
The Strange Lives of Familiar Insects
(1899–1980, American naturalist, teacher, writer)

*A*ccording to the record of the rocks, insects preceded man on this planet by quite some time, and pessimists contend that they will be the last to leave it.

Roger B. Swain
(b. 1949, biologist, TV show host)

*T*he butterfly counts not months but moments and has time enough.

Rabindranath Tagore
(Hindu poet, mystic)

*Y*ou rise early in the morning and go outdoors to make a before breakfast circuit of the house and snuff the garden air ingrained with gold. But though you think yourself taking the day by the prime, it is already old to the birds.

Christopher Morley
(1890–1957, American poet, essayist)

*S*weet bird, that shunn'st the noise of folly,
Most musical and melancholy!

John Milton
(1608–1674, English poet)

I have often tried to understand how so many deer,
and wild sheep, and bears, and flocks of grouse—
nature's cattle and poultry—could be allowed to run
at large through the mountain gardens without in any
way marring their beauty. I was therefore all the more
watchful of this feeding flock, and carefully examined
the garden after they left, to see what flowers had suffered; but I could not detect the slightest disorder,
much less destruction. It seemed rather that, like gardeners, they had been keeping it in order.

John Muir,
South of Yosemite
(1838–1896 American conservationist)

121

$\mathcal{W}$e once had a lily here that bore 108 flowers on one stalk: it was photographed naturally for all the gardening papers. The bees came from miles and miles, and there were the most disgraceful Bachanalian scenes: bees hardly able to find their way home.

Edith Sitwell
(1887–1964, British poet, writer)

$\mathcal{T}$here's a theory circulating among my friends and neighbors that I don't rise up and do battle against the creeping, crawling, hopping, flying, boring, sucking wildlife that makes free with my garden because I'm either too lazy or too squeamish.

And while there's an element of truth in this theory, it's not the whole truth. The whole truth is that I'm too ignorant and too scared. I don't know enough about insect life to dare to tamper with it . . . much.

Celestine Sibley, b. 1917,
The Sweet Apple Gardening Book

$\mathcal{W}$oodchucks are as fond of the fruits of our garden as we are, and even better at harvesting them. I've found these fat rodents will give everything but onions a taste—and I'm sure that out there somewhere is a woodchuck that likes onions in its salad.

Ruth Page,
Ruth Page's Gardening Journal
(radio show host)

$\mathcal{E}$very object . . . is emanating something . . . whether it's what's happening between you and me or what's happening between two leaves on a plant, there is something happening.

Russell Page
(1906–1985, British garden designer)

$\mathcal{S}$omewhere I read that turkeys are highly recommended as garden police. And if they eat *their* weight in bugs, as birds are said to do, it would be an orgy to end all orgies.

Celestine Sibley, b. 1917,
The Sweet Apple Gardening Book

$\mathcal{B}$ut it does seem to me that we have an obligation to know what we're doing, whom we are killing, when we grab up a bottle of spray or a packet of lethal dust. It's perfectly obvious that without insect life on earth things would come to a pretty pass. There might not be any vegetation at all. And although I don't for a minute imagine that my ninety-eight-cent can of poison spray will annihilate a whole species of insect and thereby throw what the ecologists call "the totality of interrelationships" out of kilter, I do worry that I might kill villains and heroes indiscriminately, repay the kindness of my invaluable friends, the birds, with a case of acute gastritis and possibly even jeopardize the health and well-being of those great gardening assistants, my grandchildren.

Celestine Sibley, b. 1917,
The Sweet Apple Gardening Book

To the naturalist, gardens are simply botanical paradises which attract zoological activity. As an antidote to our preoccupation with commercial interests and the indiscriminate use of herbicides, wildlife gardens will help protect life on earth. It is never too late to start.

John Feltwell, Introduction,
The Naturalist's Garden
(English author, naturalist, broadcaster)

Ladybugs work hard for us in the garden, and there's no charge. Whoever taught youngsters to chant "ladybug, ladybug, fly away home" was definitely not a gardener.

Ruth Page,
Ruth Page's Gardening Journal
(radio show host)

A weed is any plant that is growing in the wrong place.

Rosalind Creasy,
Cooking from the Garden
(cookbook writer)

Hyacinth, primrose fade from sight,
Through dusk to darkness anthems thriss,
My garden rings with new delight
When blackbirds sing into the night.

Eric Parker
(1870–1955, poet)

124

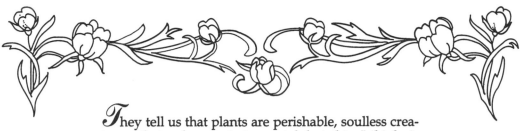

They tell us that plants are perishable, soulless creatures, that only man is immortal, but this, I think, is something that we know very nearly nothing about.

John Muir,
A Thousand Mile Walk To the Gulf
(1838–1914, American naturalist)

The best I can find to say of these coarse rampageous violets is that they will thrive anywhere and make unobtrusive masses in any cool, good soil.

Reginald Farrer
(1880–1920, garden writer)

The summer world is the insect world. Like it or not, that is how it is. There are few insects that ever find the day too hot.

Donald Culross Peattie
(1898–1964, botanist)

Managing pests means using a variety of preventive tactics to outwit insects and other pests before they damage your plants.

Rodale's Chemical Free Yard and Garden

Every insect has a mortal enemy. Cultivate that enemy and he will do your work for you.

Eleanor Perenyi, b. 1918
Green Thoughts: A Writer in the Garden

There are many bees, small wild solitary bees, that will take only the nectar of certain short-lived and local wild flowers . . . And often the flower must wait for this one right consummation, out of a world of flitting insect wings.

Donald Culross Peattie
(1898–1964, botanist)

The garden is something of a chameleon. You turn on the sprinklers and realize, from the way the barn swallows are flapping their wings on the top of the fence posts, that they think it is their shower.

Anne Raver
(columnist)

Without the microorganisms at work in compost, soil would literally be dead.

Eleanor Perenyi, b. 1918
Green Thoughts: A Writer in the Garden

The more I garden, the less I care about the death of an individual plant. I am far more interested in what caused its death and the swirl of life that is thriving inside—and outside my garden.

Anne Raver
(columnist)

The soil is not, as many suppose, a dead, inert substance. It is very much alive and dynamic. It teems with bacteria, actinomycetes, fungi, molds, yeasts, protozoa, algae and other minute organisms.

J. I. Rodale,
Pay Dirt
(1898–1971, garden writer)

To me, the garden is a doorway to other worlds; one of them, of course, is the world of birds.

Anne Raver
(columnist)

Very few of the species you see in your garden are pests.

Rodale's Chemical Free Yard and Garden

Chapter 4
Season's Cycle

$\mathcal{N}$ovember is the most disagreeable month in the whole year.

> Louisa May Alcott
> (American writer)

$\mathcal{T}$here are evenings . . . when the world is as nearly unlovely as it ever can be under natural conditions: the air cold with a sudden chill that bites worse than frost; land and sky wrapped in a dim cloud without form or motion; the year altogether at its worst, foul from the winter, frostbitten, flood-swept, sunk in a sapless lethargy when it is more than time for the stir-rings of the yearly miracle of repair.

> Anonymous,
> from "Corners of Old Grey Gardens"

$\mathcal{B}$lossom of the almond trees,
April's gift to April's bees,
Birthday ornament of spring.

> Sir Edwin Arnold
> (1832–1904,
> English poet, journalist)

$\mathscr{T}$hose manuals of make-believe, the seed catalogues, have one weakness: they don't tell me how to sustain my April gardening enthusiasm through the heat of July.

Oren Arnold,
as quoted by Reader's Digest,
July 1953

$\mathscr{C}$an anything compare to the sight of the first yellow violets blooming along a woodland path?

Howard Ensign Evans
(b. 1919, writer, teacher)

$\mathscr{N}$ow is the deyday of summer,
The full, warm robust middle age of the year,
The earth, ripe with products as well as promise.

Daniel Grayson (poet)

$\mathscr{A}$utumn carries more gold in its pocket than all the other seasons.

Jim Bishop (writer)

$\mathscr{A}$ll through the long winter I dream of my garden. On the first warm day of spring I dig my fingers deep into the soft earth. I can feel its energy, and my spirits soar.

Helen Hayes
(b. 1900, American actress)

There was something frantic in their blooming, as if they knew that frost was near and then the bitter cold. They'd lived through all the sweat and noise and stench of summertime, and now each widely opened flower was like a triumphant cry, "We will, we will make seed before we die."

Harriette Arnow, 1908–1986,
The Dollmaker

Their smiles,
Wan as primroses gather'd at midnight
By chilly finger'd spring.

John Keats,
"Endymion"
(1795–1821, English poet)

How roses age and wither with their birth;
Yea, while I speak, the flower with
crimson crouched
Hath fallen and shed her gloves on the ground.

Decimus Magnus Ausonius
(c. 310–c. 395 A.D., Roman poet)

God gave us our memories so that we might have roses in December.

James Matthew Barrie
(1860–1937, Scottish novelist, dramatist)

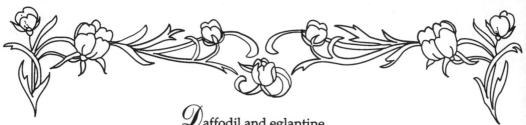

*D*affodil and eglantine,
And woodbine,
Lily, violet, and rose
Plentiful in April fair,
To the air,
Their pretty petals to unclose.

Remy Belleau
(1528–1577, poet)

*S*ummer flowers distract us with well upon a hundred families . . . autumn flowers are . . . almost wholly the tall rank composites. But something in the spring flora, perfect in its simplicity and unity, carries us back to Arcady.

Donald Culross Peattie,
An Almanac for Moderns
(1898–1964, American botanist)

*T*he dandelion tells me when to look for the swallow, the dog-toothed violet when to expect the woodthrush, and when I have found the wake-robin in bloom I know the season is fairly begun.

John Burroughs,
Wake-Robin
(1837–1921, American naturalist)

*S*pring being a tough act to follow, God created June.

Al Bernstein
(writer, columnist)

After how many illnesses such as this have I taken my first convalescent walk on the sunny terrace and always at this time of year when the honeysuckle leaves were shooting green and the apricot blossoms were dawning and the daffodils in blow. But some day will come the last illness from which there will be no going out to enjoy the sweet sights and sounds of the earthly spring, the singing of the birds, the opening of the fruit blossoms, the budding dawn of green leaves, and the blowing of the March daffodils. May I then be prepared to enter into the everlasting spring and to walk among the birds and flowers of paradise.

Frances Kilvert
(1840–1879, clergyman)

As a child, I viewed the wild field flowers, and cropped them with delight; as a young botanist, culled with rapture the various species, returning often and again to my almost exhaustless treasure in the copse; and ever now in the "sere" and "yellow leaf," when, in some mild vernal evening, I stroll through the grove, see the same floral splendor which year after year has been spread before me, I mark it with admiration and surprise, find it enchanting still, and fancy the present loveliness superior to all that has been before.

John Knapp Leonard
(soldier, illustrator, writer)

To watch the upthrust of a daffodil, to see it take form as a flower-to-be, to see the bud grow and take on the warmth of color—there is the very synthesis of spring.

Hal Borland, 1900–1978,
Hal Borland's Book of Days

$\mathscr{C}$an words describe the fragrance of the very breath of spring—that delicious commingling of the perfume of arbutus, the odor of pines, and snow-soaked soil just warming into life? Those who know the flower only as it is sold in the city streets, tied with wet dirty string into tight bunches, withered and forlorn can have little idea of the joy of finding the pink, pearly blossoms freshly opened among the withered leaves of oak and chestnut, moss, and pine needles in which they nestle close to the cold earth in the leafless, windy northern forest.

Neltje Blanchan,
Nature's Garden

$\mathscr{I}$f thou art solicitous how is the seed-time
If thou hast hope that thou mayest take the harvest,
If thou hast an eye to wisdom and deliberation
      as to the garden
Act now when the ant of the grave has not
      devoured thine eye.

Sadi (thirteenth-century Persian poet)

$\mathscr{E}$verybody should own a tree at this time of year. Or a valley full of trees, or a whole hillside. Not legally, not in the formal way . . . but in the way that one comes to own a tree by seeing it at the turn of the road, or down the street, or in a park and watching it day after day, and seeing color come to its leaves. That way it is your tree whenever you choose to pass that way, and neither fence nor title can take it from you. And it will be your tree as long as you remember.

Hal Borland
(1900–1978, writer)

Four seasons fill the measure of the year;
There are four seasons in the mind of men.

John Keats
(1795–1821, English poet)

When the hounds of spring are on winter's traces
The mother of months in meadow or plain
Fills the shadows and windy places
With crisp leaves and ripples of rain . . .

Algernon Charles Swinburne
(1837–1909, English poet)

Rivers, fountains and streams have all put on a
sweet livery of jewelled silver drops, each dresses in
new clothes, and the weather has laid aside its winter
coat.

Charles d'Orleans
(French writer)

When I behold the heavens as in their prime,
And then the earth (though old) still clad in green,
The stones and trees, insensible to time,
Nor age nor wrinkle on their front are seen;
If winter come, and greenness then do fade,
A Spring returns, and they more youthful made;
But Man grows old, lied down, remains where
            once he's laid.

Anne Bradstreet
(c. 1612–1672, English poet)

*I*f winter comes, can spring be far behind?

Percy Bysshe Shelley
(1792–1822, English poet)

*H*e places a seed in the dust for the reason
That it may in the day of distress, give fruit.

Sadi
(thirteenth-century Persian poet)

*I*n the bleak mid-winter
Frosty wind made moan,
Earth stood hard as iron,
Water like a stone;
Snow had fallen, snow on snow,
In bleak mid-winter, long ago.

Christina Georgina Rossetti
"Mid-Winter"
(1830–1894, British poet)

*B*eneath the crisp and wintry carpet hid a million
buds but stay their blossoming; and trustful birds
have built their nests amid the shuddering boughs,
and only wait to sing till one soft shower from the
south shall bid, and hither tempt the pilgrim steps of
spring.

Robert Bridges
(1844–1930, English poet)

The time
Cracks into furious flower. Lifts its face
all unashamed. And sways in wicked grace.

Gwendolyn Brooks
(b. 1917, American poet, novelist)

Despite March's windy reputation, winter isn't really blown away; it is washed away, it flows down all the hills, goes swirling down the valleys and spills out to sea. Like so many of this earth's elements, winter itself is soluble in water.

New York Times
editorial, March 17, 1964

Summer afternoon—summer afternoon; to me those have always been the two most beautiful words in the English language.

Henry James
(1843–1916, American novelist)

Such a starved bank of moss
Till, that May-morn,
Blue ran the flash across:
Violets were born!

Robert Browning
(1812–1889, English poet)

$\mathcal{S}$o simple, so humble, yet so brave. It comes before the crocus dares. I love the snowdrop, the first of all flowers, the harbinger of spring. God's New Year's gift to the earth, the fair maid of February, the daughter of the earth and the snow.

Francis Kilvert
(1840–1879, clergyman)

$\mathcal{G}$lorious are the woods in their latest gold
　　and crimson,
Yet our full-leaved willows are in their freshest green.
Such a kindly autumn, so mercifully dealing
With the growths of summer, I never yet have seen.

William Cullen Bryant
(1794–1878, American poet)

$\mathcal{I}$ always think that this month the prophet of spring brings many beautys to the landscape though a careless observer would laugh at me for saying so who believes that it brings nothing because he does not give himself the trouble to seek them.

John Clare
(1793–1864, poet)

$\mathcal{S}$pring in a garden is as irresistible, as incredible, as spring in the heart of the wilderness.

Herbert Ravenel Sass,
Adventures in Green Places
(American nature writer)

The garden, mimic of spring, is gay with flowers.

Dorothy Wordsworth
(1771–1855, writer)

Loveliest of lovely things are they,
One earth, that soonest pass away.
The rose that lives its little hour
Is prized beyond the sculptured flower.

William Cullen Bryant
(1794–1878, American poet)

The melancholy days are come, the saddest of the year,
Of wailing winds, and naked wood and meadows
      brown and sere.
Heaped in the hollows of the grove, the autumn
      leaves lie dead;
They rustle to the eddying gust, and to the rabbit's tread;
The robin and the wren are flown, and from the shrubs
      the jay,
And from the wood-top calls the crow through all the
      gloomy day.

William Cullen Bryant
(1794–1878, American poet)

I wandered lonely as a cloud
That floats on high e'er vales and hills,
When all at once I saw a crowd,
A host of golden daffodils;
Beside the lake, beneath the trees,
Fluttering and dancing in the breeze.

William Wordsworth,
"The Daffodils of Spring"
(English poet)

Though many a flower in the wood is waking,
The daffodil is our doorside queen;
She pushes upward the sword already,
To spot with sunshine the early green.

William Cullen Bryant
(1794–1878, American poet)

I am often rather saddened when I visit people and their gardens at winter. But not for the most obvious reasons: it is not the overcast sky, the rain, sleet or snow, the biting cold or any of the other features of winter's well-known charm that I find depressing. It is because all too often the garden itself has been forgotten; put away from thought, heart and deed with the last setting of the summer's sun.

Stefan Buczacki,
Conran's Basic Book of Home Gardening
(English garden writer, broadcaster

There are winter days so full of sudden sunlight that they will cheat the wise crocus into squandering its gold before its time.

Oscar Wilde (Irish poet, dramatist)

It is the month of June,
The month of leaves and roses,
When pleasant sights salute the eyes
And pleasant scents the noses.

Nathaniel Parker Willis
(1806–1867, American poet, dramatist)

*E*very season is different in the garden and one of gardening's greatest appeals is the changes in the forms, colors and perfumes that mark the passage of the year in a dynamic and continually interesting manner.

Stefan Buczacki,
Conran's Basic Book of Home Gardening
(English garden writer, broadcaster)

I hear the birds singing sweetly through the woods. You can see flowers blooming through the grass. A hint of early summer, with heather now in flower and roses red.

Gotfrit Von Wifen (writer)

*F*or the urban population spring is heralded by less celestial signs—not a wedge of geese in the sky, but a span of new plucked terriers on the avenue, or a potted hyacinth groomed for April.

E. B. White
(1899–1985, American essayist)

*H*ow friendly the pine-tree is to man—so docile and available as timber and so warm and protective as shelter. Its balsam is salve to his wounds, its fragrance is long life to his nostrils; an abiding perennial tree, tempering the climate, cool as murmuring waters in summer and like a wrapping of fur in winter.

John Burroughs
(1837–1921, American naturalist)

*Y*oung meadows hasting their green laps to fill with golden dandelion and daffodils: these are fit sights for spring.

Clarence Chatham Cook (writer)

*T*he sharp taste of the first radish has scarcely left my lips when the first tomato of the season is ready to eat. It hardly seems fair!

Phyllis Rosenblum,
Albany Times Union
(garden columnist)

A successful garden in spring and summer bloom is a collection of delights.

Josephine Von Miklos
and Evelyn Fiore, 1900–1972,
The History, the Beauty, the Riches
of the Gardener's World

*N*ow Khrinketh rose and lily flower,
That whilen bore that sweet savour,
In summer that sweet tide.

Geoffrey Chaucer
(c. 1342–1400, English poet)

*S*pring is sooner recognized by plants than by men.

Chinese proverb

I love the fall. I love it because of the smells that you speak of; and also because things are dying, things that you don't have to take care of any more, and the grass stops growing.

Mark Van Doren
(1894–1972, American writer)

*N*ow sol o'ercomes old winter's frowns,
And soon unlocks the frozen grounds,
So drink March out with season'd mead,
To flavor every new year deed.

Unknown,
from Farmer's Almanac

*S*pring flowers, I have observed, look best in the day, and by sunshine.

Samuel Taylor Coleridge
(1772–1834, writer)

*A*utumn arrives, array'd in splendid mien;
Vines cluster'd full, add to the beauteous scene,
And fruit trees cloth'd profusely laden, nod,
Compliant bowing to the fertile sod.

Unknown,
from Farmer's Almanac

*F*allen leaves lying on the grass in November bring more happiness than the daffodils.

Cyril Connolly
(1903–1974, English essayist, novelist)

143

The piercing cold commands us shut the door, and rouse the cheerful hearth; for at the heels of dark November comes with arrowy scourge the tyrannous December.

Unknown,
from Allen's Almanack

Sidnaeian showers
Of sweet discourse, whose powers
Can crown old Winter's head with flowers.

Richard Crashau
(1613–1649, English poet)

When April blows his horn
It's good for hay and corn.

Unknown

Clean air; bird song; fresh flowers; and the leaves unfurling on the twigs.

Pierre D'Alverne
(French poet)

O gallant flowering May,
Which month is painter of the world,
As some great clerks to day.

Unknown

The osiers are in bud, the tops of the trees are tipped with bloom, the leaves are green; and from the depths of the green come bird voice and song.

Arnaut Daniel
(1180–1200, French writer)

The winter sap resembles me,
Whose sap lies in the root,
The spring draws nigh, as it, so I
Shall bud, I hope, and shoot.

Unknown

In autumn's cup lingers a cloudy wine in which spring's roses must shed their petals.

Ruben Dario
(1867–1916, Spanish writer)

Every autumn your mellow leaves fall in waves, like a winter cloak on your native hillside.

Victor De Laprade
(French writer)

Noon, that summer king, spread over the plain, falls in silver sheets from the nights of the blue sky. Everything is quiet. The air blazes and burns breathlessly. The earth drowses in its fiery robe.

Leconte de Lisle
(French writer)

$\mathcal{M}$y spring appears, Oh see what here doth grow.

Sir Philip Sydney
(1554–1586, poet)

$\mathcal{N}$ow it is summer, and as usual, life fills me with transport and I forget to work. This year I have struggled for a long time, but the beauty of the world has conquered me.

Leo Tolstoy
(1828–1910, Russian writer)

$\mathcal{R}$oses white and red bloomed upon the spray;
One opened, leaf by leaf, to greet the morn,
Shyly at first, then in sweet disarray;
Another, yet a youngling, newly born,
Scarce struggled from the bud.

Lorenzo de' Medici
(fifteenth-century Italian philosopher, writer)

$\mathcal{W}$hen the woods and groves are covered with green, and grass and flowers appear in the orchards and meadows, and the birds who were sad are now gay among the foliage, then I also sing and exalt, I bloom again and flourish, as is my wont.

Bernard de Ventadour
(writer)

$\mathcal{T}$hus potently the year ends with golden wine and garden fruits. Around us the woodlands are silently wonderful and are the companions of the solitary.

Georg Trakl
(1887–1914, writer)

$\mathcal{F}$or winter's rains and ruins are over,
And all the season of snows and sins;
The days dividing loves and lover
The light that loses, the night that wins;
And time remembered is grief forgotten,
And forests are slain and flowers begotten,
And in the green underwood and cover
Blossom by blossom the spring begins.

Algernon Charles Swinburne,
"Atlanta in Calydon"
(1837–1909, English poet)

147

There are still flowers, tied up in fine bunches, from the last glories of summer.

Fritz Diettrich
(German writer)

One of the innate perversities of nature is that the longest day of the year occurs well before half-time in the growing season.

Roger B. Swain,
The Practical Gardener
1989 (biologist, TV show host)

Just when winter appears interminable, and it seems not one more bleak and bitter day can be endured, the first harbinger of the gardener's spring arrives: the nursery catalogues!

Martha Smith,
Beds I Have Known, *1990*

Rise up, my love, my fair one, and come away.
For, lo, the winter is past, the rain is over
       and gone;
The flowers appear on the earth; the time of
       the singing birds is
come, and the voice of the turtle is heard in
       our land.

Song of Solomon 2:10–12

*W*hen daisies go shall winter time
Silver the simple grass with rime.

Robert Louis Stevenson
(1850–1894, Scottish poet, novelist, essayist)

*T*he garden is very forlorn, swept by chill winds, plunged into the frigid temperatures of dead winter. Most color has left the landscape; in its place is a palette of grisaille tones. The last outdoor task, wrapping the roses and perennial borders in burlap, is accomplished. All at once I have time and reason to concentrate on beautifying my house, filling it with living plants and flowers.

Martha Stewart,
Martha Stewart's Gardening Month by Month, *1991*
(American life-style writer, magazine editor)

*I*like flowering plants, but I like trees more—for the reason, I suppose, that they are slower coming to maturity, are longer lived, that you can become better acquainted with them, and that in the course of years memories and associations hang as thickly on their boughs as do leaves in summer or fruit in autumn.

Alexander Smith, 1830–1867,
contributor to Corners of Grey Old Gardens

*A*ll the seasons run their race
In this quiet resting place;
Peach and apricot and fig
Here will ripen and grow big.

Henry Austin Dobson
(1840–1921, English poet)

149

*S*ee where the farmer with a master's eye,
Surveys his little kingdom and exults
In sovereign independence . . .
Here stacks of hay, there pyramids of corn,
Promise the future market large supplies:
While with an eye of triumph he surveys
His piles of wood, and laughs at winter's frown.

Robert Dodsley
(1703–1764, English poet, dramatist)

. . . *A*nd the spring arose on the garden fair,
Like the spirit of love felt everywhere;
And each flower and herb on earth's dark breast
Rose from the dreams of its wintry rest.

Percy Bysshe Shelley
(1792–1822, English poet)

*H*ere's flowers for you; hot lavender, mints, savory,
marjoram; the marigold, that goes to bed with the
sun, and with him rises weeping: these are flowers of
middle summer, and I think they are given to men of
middle age.

William Shakespeare
(1564–1616, English dramatist, poet)

*O*h, leaf, that yesterday was green
But now is blushing rosy red,
What happened to you overnight?
Why not to me, instead?

Doris Black (poet)

(On spring:)

*W*hen daisies pied and violets blue
And lady-smocks all silver white
And cuckoo-buds of yellow hue
Do paint the meadows with delight.

William Shakespeare
(1564–1616, English dramatist, poet)

*N*othing in this world is really precious until we
know that it will soon be gone. The lily, the starry daffodil, the regal irises . . . are the lovelier for their immi-
nent vanishing. The snow crystal has but touched
earth ere it begins to die.

Donald Culross Peattie,
An Almanac for Moderns
(1898–1964, American botanist)

*T*hey are the lords and owners of their faces,
Others but stewards of their excellence.
The summer's flower is to the summer sweet,
Though to itself it only live and die.

William Shakespeare
(1564–1616, English dramatist, poet)

*A*nd jealousy it is that kills
This world when all
The spring's behaviours here is spent
To make the world magnificent.

John Drinkwater
(1882–1937, English poet, dramatist)

I would I had some flowers O' the spring, that might
Become your time of day; and yours, and yours . . .

William Shakespeare,
The Winter's Tale
(1564–1616, English dramatist, poet)

S afe in the earth they lie, serenely waiting;
They never speak to north winds or to snow,
Perfume and color in the dark creating,
Fit for the sunlit world that they will know.

Louise Driscoll,
"Bulbs"
(American poet)

H ark! Hark! The lark at heaven's gate sings,
And Phoebus 'gins arise,
His steeds to water at those springs
Oh chaliced flowers that lies;
And winking Mary-buds begin
To open their golden eyes:
With everything that pretty is
My lady sweet, arise.

William Shakespeare
(1564–1616, English poet, dramatist)

T he country habit has me by the heart,
For his bewitched for ever who has seen,
not with his eyes but with his vision, Spring,
Flow down the woods and stipple leaves with sun.

Vita Sackville-West
(1892–1962, English poet, novelist)

$\mathcal{T}$o everything there is a season, and a time to every purpose under heaven.
A time to be born, and a time to die; a time to plant, and a time to pluck up that which is planted . . .

Ecclesiastes 3:1–2

$\mathcal{S}$elf-sown my stately garden grows;
The winds and wind-blown seed,
Cold April rain and colder snows
My hedges plant and feed.

Ralph Waldo Emerson
(1803–1882, American philosopher, writer)

$\mathcal{T}$he wine that has been made to bear fruit in the spring, withers and dies before autumn.

Jean-Jacques Rousseau
(1712–1778, Swiss philosopher)

$\mathcal{D}$o what we can, summer will have its flies.

Ralph Waldo Emerson
(1803–1882, American philosopher, writer)

$\mathcal{I}$n my Autumn garden I was fain
To mourn among my scattered roses;
Alas for that last rosebud which uncloses
To Autumn's languid sun and rain
When all the world is on the wane!

Christina Georgina Rossetti
(1830–1894, British poet)

*E*arth laughs in flowers.

Ralph Waldo Emerson
(1803–1882, American philosopher, writer)

*D*oesn't it seem as if autumn were the real creator, more creative then spring, which all at once is, more creative, when it comes with its will to change and destroys the much too finished, much too satisfied, indeed almost bourgeois comfortable picture of summer.

Rainer Maria Rilke
(1875–1926, Austrian poet)

*H*ope, patience, and work—these are the three graces of spring.

Ruth Shaw Ernst,
The Naturalist's Garden

*O*f course everything is blooming most recklessly; if it were voices instead of colors, there would be an unbelievable shrieking into the heart of the night.

Rainer Maria Rilke
(1875–1926, Austrian poet)

*B*ut now in September the garden has cooled, and with it my possessiveness. The sun warms my back instead of beating on my head. No longer blindingly bright, it throws things before me into sharp relief and deepening color. The harvest has dwindled, and I have grown apart from the intense midsummer relationship that brought it on.

Robert Finch,
Common Ground *(naturalist)*

*T*he garden air is full of the sound of crickets, the year's clock made audible, ticking off the days. I have learned that it is the black field crickets that have eaten my tomatoes in late summer, but there is still such a red flood ripening on the window sills that I do not begrudge them what they take now.

Robert Finch,
Common Ground *(naturalist)*

*I*s there anything more soothing than the quiet whir of a lawnmower on a summer afternoon?

F. Scott Fitzgerald
(1896–1940, American novelist)

155

*O*ut of one wintry twig,
   One bud
   One blossom's worth of warmth
At long last.

> *Ranstu,*
> *a haiku from* Haiku Harvest
> *(Oriental poet)*

*T*all tulips lift in scarlet tire
Brimming the April dusk with fire.

> *Lizette Woodworth Reese*
> *(1856–1935, American poet)*

*S*pring makes everything young again except man.

> *Jean Paul Richter*
> *(1763–1825, German novelist, aesthetician)*

*O*ne speaks of the moods of spring, but the days that are her true children have only one mood; they are all full of the rising and dropping of winds, and the whistling of birds. New flowers may come out, the green embroidery of the hedges increase, but the same heaven broods overhead, soft thick, and blue, the same figures, seen and unseen, are wandering by coppice and meadow.

> *E. M. Forster,*
> Howard's End
> *(1879–1970, English novelist)*

The marigolds were planted late this year, but they seem more fitting as autumn flowers, when all things, even sunsets, eschew pastels. The garden is like a fire going out, dying from its center, but burning clear to the last.

Robert Finch,
Common Ground
(naturalist)

They are not long, the days of wine and roses:
Out of a misty dream
Our path emerges for a while, then closer
Within a dream.

Ernest Powson (poet)

Fruit out of season, sorrow out of reason.

Henry Friend,
Flowers and Fruit Lore

But each spring . . . a gardening instinct, sore as the sap rising in the trees, stirs within us. We look about and decide to tame another little bit of ground.

Lewis Gannett
(1891–1966, writer)

My "drinking uncle" says that, even during the worst blizzard in January, a glass of dandelion wine will bring summer right into the house.

Euell Gibbons, 1911–1975,
Stalking the Wild Asparagus

*A*round here, we call tulips the "lipsticks of the garden" because their rich colors and elegant flowers give the spring border that final touch that brings it to life.

Amos Pettingill
(1901–1981, writer)

I wish a month like April were more aware of what we expect from it.

Beryl Pfizer,
as quoted in Reader's Digest,
April 1972 (writer)

*W*hen swelling buds their od'rous foliage shed,
And gently harden into fruit, the wise
Spare not the little offsprings, if they grow
Redundant.

John Philips
(1676–1709, English poet)

*S*itting with quiet, folded hands, content
　　　　and peaceful
And smiling a mysterious promise,
My winter garden waits.

Caroline Giltinan
(American poet)

*E*very year, back spring comes, with nasty little birds yapping their fool heads off, and the ground all mucked up with arbutus.

Dorothy Parker
(1893–1967, American poet, satirist)

*C*uttings taken in the spring will root readily in moist peat moss. Plant them in a cold frame in the fall and transplant them to their permanent locations the following spring. Before too long your garden should rival the woods in autumn glory.

Jeanne Goode,
Horticulture Magazine,
September 1986

*T*he meanest floweret of the vale,
The simplest note that swells the gale,
The common sun, the air, the skies,
To him are opening paradise.

Thomas Gray
(1716–1771, English poet)

*F*irst, it's a shy gleam of crocus against melting March snow, then a yellow blaze of daffodil. The heart begins to sing, the step to lighten, because Spring is just up ahead. But when dogwood white and dogwood pink burst into radiant Chorus along the greening hillsides—then, then at last, you know Spring is really here, and here to stay.

Robert O'Brien (writer)

It's spring! Again life focuses
On grasses and on crocuses,
On rows of deep-blue irises
And one or two new viruses.

Philene Hammer,
as quoted by Reader's Digest,
April 1956

The truth is that nothing is more sprightly to see than patches of fat Dutch crocuses in March, coming as they do to lift our spirits and amaze the young and simple.

Henry Mitchell
(garden columnist)

April prepared her green traffic light, and the world thinks "Go!"

Christopher Morley
(1890–1957, American poet, essayist)

Welcome maids of honour,
You doe bring
In the Spring;
And wait upon her.

She has virgins many,
Fresh and faire;
Yet you are
More sweet than any.

Robert Herrick, "To Violets"
(1591–1674, English poet)

$\mathcal{G}$ardening will make you appreciate something that many people have grown to ignore—that we are all part of the mystery of the earth's cycle of life. No scientist in the world can make winter follow spring. It's rather a relief, don't you think? Not even politicians can tamper with the seasons! Think of what a mess they would make if they could. We wouldn't know when to plant our gardens. What confusion!

> C. Z. Guest,
> First Garden *(socialite)*

$\mathcal{N}$ow it is really a strange hot day—sudden spring. One's consciousness seems to come suddenly out of its sheath—like a bud hurried in a stalk that suddenly comes out and there is a flower—wide open.

> *Katharine Butler Hathaway (writer)*

$\mathcal{T}$here is nothing like the first hot days of spring when the gardener stops wondering if it's too soon to plant the dahlias and starts wondering if it's too late.

> *Henry Mitchell,*
> The Essential Earthman
> *(garden columnist)*

$\mathcal{O}$h, little rose tree, bloom!
Summer is nearly over.
The dahlias bleed, and the phlox is seed.
Nothing's left of the clover.
And the path of the poppy no one knows.
I would blossom if I were a rose.

> *Edna St. Vincent Millay*
> *(1829–1950, poet)*

161

$\mathcal{G}$ather ye rosebuds while ye may,
Old Time is still a-flying,
And this same flower that smiles today
Tomorrow will be dying.

Robert Herrick
(1591–1674, English poet)

$\mathcal{W}$hen apple seeds, all white before,
Begin to darken in the core,
I know that summer, scarcely here,
Is gone until another year.

Edna St. Vincent Millay
(1892–1950, poet)

. . . $\mathcal{W}$hat can be more delightful in spring, in the excursion of the walks, than the charming appearance which the [espalier] trees make when covered with their showy bloom, differing in themselves, in those of different genera, species, and varieties; or in summer, to see the fruit of the different sorts advancing to perfection and in autumn to arrive successively to maturity?

Bernard McMahon,
McMahon's American Gardener

$\mathcal{W}$oe is me! When winter comes, where shall I find the flowers, the sunshine, and the shady places? The walls stand speechless and cold. The weather cocks, angles in the wind.

Friedrich Holderlin
(German poet)

In spring for sheer delight,
I set the lanterns swinging through the trees,
Bright as the myriad argosies of night,
That ride the clouded billows of the sky.
Red dragons leap and plunge in gold and silver seas,
And, O my garden gleaming cold and white,
Thou hast outshone the far faint moon on high.

Yüan Mee
(Oriental poet)

The autumn day reclines in its rich plenty.

Friedrich Holderlin
(German poet)

When I visit a garden center in September, I get the uneasy feeling that every flower in the world has a rounded form. Chrysanthemums have become events rather than garden plants.

Frederick McGourty, Jr.,
American Horticulturist Magazine,
February 1985
(American horticulturist)

Yellow japanned buttercups and star-disked dandelions—just as we see them lying in the grass, like sparks that have leaped from the kindling sun of summer.

Oliver Wendell Holmes, Sr.
(1841–1935, American poet)

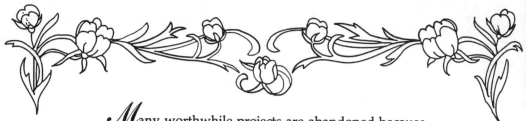

*M*any worthwhile projects are abandoned because the energy of a gardener in August does not match his aspirations of the preceding April.

> *Frederick McGourty, Jr.,*
> *Brooklyn Botanic Garden Record Handbook:*
> *"Gardening with Wildflowers"*
> *(American horticulturist)*

*A*utumn the bringer of fruit, has poured out her riches, and soon sluggish winter returns.

> *Horace*
> *(65–8 B.C., Latin poet)*

*B*lessed is he who takes comfort in seed time and harvest, setting the warfare of life to the hymn of the seasons.

> *J. W. Howe*
> *(1819–1910, American poet)*

*W*hile June gardens are full of the masses of gaudy roses and daylilies we love so much, a more subtle show is going on in southern woods and fields. Millions of tiny white umbrellas make up the big white parasols of Queen Anne's Lace, in bloom now for nearly a month.

> *William Lanier Hunt,*
> Southern Gardens, Southern Gardening

A spell lies on the Garden. Summer sits.
With finger on her lips as if she heard
The steps of Autumn echo on the hill.

Gertrude Huntington McGiffert
(writer)

*L*ately, I have had a special interest in extending the period in which the garden is attractive further into autumn. Normal people admire sugar maples or watch football games in fall. My taste runs more toward combating seasonal senescence in the garden, delaying the inevitable, and more positively, preserving beauty.

Frederick McGourty, Jr.,
American Horticulturist Magazine,
February 1985
(American horticulturist)

*B*uttercups and daisies
Oh, the pretty flowers;
Coming ere the springtime,
To tell of sunny hours.

Mary Howitt
(English poet)

*T*here is greater relish for the earliest fruit of the season.

Martial, "Epigrams"
(first-century Latin poet)

I hate to be reminded of the passage of time, and in a garden of flowers one can never escape from it. It is one of the charms of a garden of grass and evergreens, that there for a while one is allowed to hug the illusion that time carries.

E. V. Lucus (writer)

*T*he exuding beauty of the earth, in her splendour of life, yields a new thought with every petal . . . These are only hours that are not wanted—these hours that absorb the sour and fill it with beauty. This is real life, and all else is illusion, or mere endurance.

Richard Jeffries
(1848–1887, English naturalist, novelist)

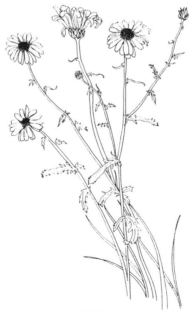

*S*pring flowers are long since gone. Summer's bloom hangs limp on every terrace. The gardener's feet drag a bit on the dusty path and the hinge in his back is full of creaks.

Louise Seymour Jones,
Put a Feather in Your Hat

*L*ilacs
False blue,
White,
Purple,
Colour of lilac,
Your great puffs of flowers
Are everywhere in this my New England
Among your heart-shaped leaves
Orange orioles hop like music-box birds and sing
Their little weak soft songs;
In the crooks of your branches
The bright eyes of song sparrows sitting on
       spotted eggs
Peer restlessly through the light and shadow
      of all springs.

Amy Lowell
(1874–1925, American poet, essayist)

A garden is a lovely thing
That must be spaded in the spring
Weeded when the summer's searing
Mulched in Fall when Winter's nearing.
Of all the seasons do you wonder
I like it best when it's snowed under?

Glen Lorang (writer)

*S*hed no tear! O shed no tear!
The flower will bloom another year.
Weep no more! O weep no more!
Young buds sleep in the root's white core.

John Keats
(1795–1821, English poet)

*A*ugust brings the ears of corn,
Then the harvest home is born.

Sarah Loleridge
(American poet)

*O*n this June day the buds in my garden are almost
as enchanting as the open flowers. Things in bud
bring, in the heat of a June Noontide, the recollection
of the loveliest days of the year—those days of May
when all is suggested, nothing yet fulfilled.

Mrs. Francis King,
The Well-Considered Garden

*M*ay and June. Soft syllables, gentle names for the
two best months in the garden year: cool, misty mornings gently burned away with a warming spring sun,
followed by breezy afternoons and chilly nights. The
discussion of philosophy is over, it's time for work to
begin.

H. Peter Loewer,
Month-by-Month Garden Almanac
(botanical author, illustrator)

*N*o one thinks of winter when the grass is green!

Rudyard Kipling
(1865–1936, English poet)

*S*eason of mists and mellow fruitfulness,
Close bosom-friend of the maturing sun;
Conspiring with him how to load and bless
With fruit the vines that round their
thatch-eaves run.

John Keats, "To Autumn"
(1795–1821, English poet)

*T*hat God once loved a garden
We learn in Holy writ.
And seeing gardens in the spring
I well can credit it.

Winifred Letts
(Irish poet, writer)

*I*n a world that daily flirts with disaster, continually teetering on the brink of hysteria, where the unbelievable has become the commonplace, and crises upon crises are flung at you from newspaper and T.V., it's very easy to lose your orientation and find yourself asking where the time has gone. But when you think of the last time you saw a violet in spring, an apple tree weighted with blossoms, or the annual display of an African amaryllis, once again you can sense the true passage of time.

H. Peter Loewer,
Bringing the Outdoors In
(botanical author, illustrator)

169

Chapter 5
Wind and Weather

(The wind:)

It's different when it rushes through the old apple-trees; it's different again when it rustles across the tops of the pine trees. It's different when it storms across the fields; and it's different when it rushes through the hedges.

Peter Altenberg (writer)

We plough the fields, and scatter
The good seed on the land,
But it is fed and watered
By God's Almighty Hand.
He sends the snow in winter,
The warmth to swell the grain,
The breezes and the sunshine,
And soft refreshing rain.

Jane Montgomery Campbell, hymn
(British hymn writer)

Heart's Ease, An herb that sometimes
  hath been seen
In my love's garden plot to flourish green,
Is dead and withered with a wind of woe;
And bitter rue in place thereof doth grow.

Anonymous

*A*wake, O north wind, and come, thou south; blow upon my garden, that the spices thereof pray flow out. Let my beloved come into the garden and eat his pleasant fruits.

Song of Solomon 4:16

*T*he ash tree growing in the corner of the garden was felled. It was lopped first: I heard the sound and looking out and seeing it maimed there came at that moment a great pang and I wished to die and not see the landscapes of the world destroyed any more.

Gerard Manley Hopkins
(1844–1889, poet)

*A*s she [the moon] cleared the tops of the trees a soft golden beam stole across the turf from between the two birches, discovering and tipping here and there a bunch of white flowers in the beds and soon the shadows of the tree stems lay across the drive and the foliage of the birches was mapped upon the lawn.

Francis Kilvert
(1840–1879, clergyman)

*W*ould you have gardens, come to me . . .
The breeze, the perfumed vagabond,
False to all else, is true to me,
And he shall heal your misery.

Anonymous

*F*aint murmurs from the pine-tops reach my ear,
As if a harp-string touched in some far sphere—
Vibrating in the lucid atmosphere,
Let the soft south wind waft its music here.

Thomas Bailey Aldrich
(American writer)

*I'*m glad the sky is painted blue;
And the earth is painted green;
And such a lot of nice fresh air
All sandwiched in between.

Anonymous

*F*rost is gold in the morning, silver in the afternoon
and lead at night.

Bishop Shute Barrington
(1678–1734, English religious writer)

*T*he narrow bud opens her beauties to
the sun, and love runs in her thrilling veins.

William Blake
(1757–1827, English poet)

. . . *T*his bright and constant flower enamoured of
the sun . . .

Marguerite Blessington
(writer)

$\mathcal{M}$y tent stands in a garden of aster and golden-rod, tilled by the rain and the sunshine, and sown by the hand of God.

William Bliss Carman
(1861–1929, Canadian poet)

$\mathcal{O}$pen the window wider, the air is so fresh and pure and calm, that the elms and the beech trees are all decked and draped, branch by branch with white snow.

Francis Viele-Griffin
(1864–1937, writer)

$\mathcal{T}$he tints of autumn—a mighty flower garden blossoming under the spell of the enchanter, Frost.

John Greenleaf Whittier
(1807–1892, American poet)

$\mathcal{T}$he stars are everywhere tonight,
Above, beneath me and around;
They fill the sky with powdery light
And glimmer from the night-strewn ground;
For where the folded daisies are
In every one I see a star.
And so I know that when I pass
Where no sun's shadow counts the hours
And where the sky was there is grass
Through the long night in which I lie
Stars will be shining in my sky.

Andrew Young, "Daisies"
(1885–1971, Scottish poet)

$\mathcal{T}$he blueberry is nature's compensation for the ruin of forest fires. It grows best where the woods have been burned away and the soil is too poor to raise another crop of trees.

Henry Van Dyke, Little Rivers
(1852–1933, American clergyman, educator)

$\mathcal{W}$eather means more when you have a garden,
There's nothing like listening to a shower and
thinking how it is
soaking in and around your lettuce and green beans.

Henry Van Dyke
(1852–1933, American clergyman, poet, essayist)

(Recounting the aftermath of a storm:)

*B*arefoot, we sloshed about in mud to our ankles, rescued tomato plants from their sunshades, which had been beaten down around them, and transplanted another row of lettuce seedlings, as much to get our hands in the warm, wet soil as to get those lettuce roots in. Then, wriggling our toes in the mud like eight-year-olds, we closed the garden gate, wiped our feet on the lawn grass, lifted our faces, eyes shut, mouths wide, drank the rain as it fell, and were one with grass and trees.

Hal Borland, 1900–1978,
Hal Borland's Book of Days

*D*elay gives strength; the tender bladed grain
Shot up to stalk can stand the wind and rain.
The tree, whose branches now are grown too big
For hand to bend, was set a tender twig.
When planted, to the slightest touch would yield,
But now has got possession of the field.

Unknown,
Farmer's Almanac

I mind me in the days departed,
How often underneath the sun
With childish bounds I used to run
To a garden long deserted.

Elizabeth Barrett Browning
(1806–1861, English poet)

The temperature rose into the eighties. No wind. Just that hot lid of humidity. It was a day to sit and do nothing, but I tried to do some work in the garden. Five minutes with a hoe and I was soaked to the skin with sweat. So I gave up, got out the riding mower and mowed the lawn and the borders of the garden. And even on the mower I sweated. But it still was a beautiful day.

Hal Borland, 1900–1978,
Hal Borland's Book of Days

(The wind:)

It sings of the savage events of time immemorial; sings, cries away, hangs at the window, kisses, and tries to break into the room. Then, weeping, it falls, plunged into despair, worn out, and strays into the right, bent in humble bowing.

Julian Tuwim
(1894–1953, Polish writer)

March winds and April showers
Bring forth May Flowers.

Unknown

The poppy's red effrontery,
Till autumn spoils its fleening quite with rain,
And portionless, a dry, brown, rattling crane
Protrudes.

Robert Browning
(1812–1889, English poet)

*P*ure as lines of green that streak the White
Of the Snowdrop's inner leaves.

Alfred, Lord Tennyson
(1809–1892, English poet)

*T*he sun stands still and flowers
Are all withdrawn, but memories
Give back cardinal Lobelia, tall
Scarlet fountains for the humming-bird—
Vines, broken with blue and silver apios—
Beside hanging horns of jewelweed,
With pods which pop when prodded
By the idle or enquiring finger.

Dylan Thomas
(1914–1953, Welsh writer)

*Y*et one smile more, departing, distant sun!
One mellow smile through the soft vapory air,
Ere, o'er the frozen earth, the loud winds run,
Or snows are sifted o'er the meadows bare.

William Cullen Bryant
(1794–1878, American poet)

*B*ut Oh! fell death's untimely frost,
That nipt my flower so early.

Robert Burns
(1759–1796, Scottish poet)

The sun shone down for nearly a week on the secret garden. The Secret Garden was what Mary called it when she was thinking of it. She liked the name, and she liked still more the feeling that when its beautiful old walls shut her in no one knew where she was. It seemed almost like being shut out of the world in some fairy place.

Frances Hodgson Burnett,
1849–1924, The Secret Garden

Give me a little plot of ground,
Where might I with the sun agree,
Though every day he walk the round
My garden he should seldom see.

James Shirley
(1596–1666, English dramatic poet)

Snowfall not only provides a general amnesty for procrastinators, but does an excellent job of whitewashing the facts. If you didn't gather up your dead tomato and squash vines, your neighbor will never know.

Roger B. Swain,
Earthly Pleasures
(biologist, TV host)

But pleasures are like poppies spread—
You seize the flow'r, its bloom is shed;
Or like the snow falls in the river—
A moment white—then meets forever.

Robert Burns
(1759–1796, Scottish poet)

The scattered flowers alone are gay;
Their fragrance fills the gentle wind,
And I, grown drowsy, dream and find
The long forgotten yesterday.

Frank Dempster Sherman
(American poet)

These flowers, which were splendid and sprightly,
Waking in the dawn of the morning,
In the evening will be a pitiful frivolity,
Sleeping in the night's cold arms.

Pedro Calderon de la Barca
(Spanish poet)

O wild west wind, thou breath of Autumn's being,
Thou, from whose unseen presence the leaves dead
Are driven, like ghosts from an enchanter fleeing,
Yellow, and black, and pale, and hectic red,
Pestilence-stricken multitudes.

Percy Bysshe Shelley,
"Ode to the West Wind"
(1792–1822, English poet)

(Rain:)

Which may have painted with his soft showers this
garden full of leaves and of flowers.

Geoffrey Chaucer, "The Franklin's Tale"
(c. 1342–1400, English poet)

The thirsty Earth soaks up the rain,
And drinks, and gapes for drink again.
The plants suck in the earth, and are
With constant drinking fresh and fair.

Abraham Cowley, "Drinking"
(1618–1667, English poet)

Daffodils,
That come before the swallow dares,
And take
The winds of March with beauty.

William Shakespeare
(1564–1616, English dramatist, poet)

A sensitive plant in a garden grew,
And the young winds fed it with silver dew,
And it opened its fan-like leaves to the light,
And closed them beneath the kisses of night.

Percy Bysshe Shelley, "The Sensitive Plant"
(1792–1822, English poet)

The evening mist in the garden is white and chill,
And all the vegetables stand in waiting rows,
They lift their formless leaves and stalks, so still,
You would say that hardly a root of them drinks,
    or grows.

Rupert Croft-Cooke
(1903–1979, poet)

When the flowers have taken wing
There's an end of gardening;
And when gardening began,
'Twas not wind made out the plan!

Geoffrey Scott
(poet)

Now I can see sombre, dark and stormy skies,
bringing gale and rain and howling gusts throughout
the land. Snow, ice and frost beset us. The sun, once
hot and strong, yields little heat; the boughs are
denuded of blossom and leaf, and no birdsong comes
from the hedges and woodlands.

Raimbaut D'Aurenga (writer)

The unseasonable cold and the heavy frost strip the
enamel and the beauty of the earth's painted landscape, and the clear skies are besmirched by dark
clouds.

Fernando De Herrera
(1534–1597, writer)

In my garden goes a fiend
Dark and wild, whose name is Wind.

Geoffrey Scott
(poet)

*P*lants are marvelously docile. When they die prematurely, it is not of "treatment" but of maltreatment, and with Orchids especially, as with women and chameleons, their life is a reflection of what is around them.

Edward Sprague Rand, Jr.
(American writer)

*W*ho has seen the wind?
Neither you nor I:
But when the trees bow down their heads,
The wind is passing by.

Christina Georgina Rossetti
(1830–1894, English poet)

The great days remain, covered in dust, lingering proud and peaceful over the level land. In their hot hands the cluster of grapes ripen, the fields turn yellow, and the gardens are scorched.

Fritz Diettrich
(German writer)

You can't forget a garden
When you have planted seed—
When you have watched the weather
And know a rose's need.

Louise Driscoll
(American poet, writer)

In the morning the whitened yard, flower beds, roofs and fences; delicate patterns on the window panes; the trees in winter silver, gay magpies outside, and the hills softly overspread with winter's brilliant carpeting. All is bright, all is white around.

Aleksandr Pushkin
(1799–1837, Russian poet)

How could sour cherries, or half-ripe strawberries or wet rosebuds, even if they do come from one's own garden, reward a man for the loss of the ease and the serene conscience of one who sings merrily in the streets, and cares not whether worms burrow, whether suns burn, whether winds overturn, whether droughts destroy, whether floods drown, whether gardens flourish or not?

Oliver Bell Dunce (writer)

*H*ow simple and rustic . . . would seem the dog-roses which in a few weeks time, would be climbing the same hillside path in the heat of the sun, dressed in the smooth silk of their blushing pink bodices, which would be undone and scattered by the first breath of wind.

Marcel Proust,
Swanns' Way
(1871–1922, French novelist)

*A*wake, O north wind; and come, thou south, blow upon my garden, that the spices there of may flow out. Let my Beloved come into his garden, and eat his pleasant fruits.

Ecclesiastes 4:16

*W*eather is the greatest uncertainty in the naturalist's garden.

Ruth Shaw Ernst,
The Naturalist's Garden
(author, naturalist)

*T*he first fall of snow is not only an event, it is a magical event. You go to bed in one kind of world and wake up in another quite different, and if this is not without enchantment then where is it to be found?

J. B. Priestly
(1894–1984, British novelist)

*T*here are no green thumbs or black thumbs. There are only gardeners and non-gardeners. Gardeners are the ones who ruin after ruin get on with the high defiance of nature herself, creating, in the very face of her chaos and tornado, the bower of roses and the pride of irises.

Henry Mitchell,
The Essential Earthman
(garden columnist)

*H*ope is a necessary ingredient in gardening, for nature is often capricious, and our best efforts may be unsuccessful or need repeating.

Ruth Shaw Ernst,
The Naturalist's Garden
(author, naturalist)

*F*or the present let the moon shine brightly and the breezes of the spring blow gently, dying away from the gale of the day, and let the earth, who brings increase, bring peace.

E. M. Forster, Howard's End
(1879–1970, English novelist)

*I*t is not nice to garden anywhere. Everywhere there are violent winds, startling once-per-five-centuries floods, unprecedented droughts, record-setting freezes, abusive and blasting heats never known before. There is no place, no garden, where these terrible things do not drive gardeners mad.

Henry Mitchell,
The Essential Earthman
(garden columnist)

*T*he frost hurts not weeds.

Thomas Fuller, M.D.
(1608–1661, English physician, writer)

A plant is a living thing. It's subject to the same rules and regulations that govern the human body. Without light, plants become anemic, without air, water, and food, they slowly waste away. Too much heat or too much cold will generally do them in. Without an occasional rest, they push themselves to an early demise, and without maintenance, they quickly appear unshaven and unshorn.

H. Peter Loewer,
Bringing the Outdoors In

*D*ews of the brightest in life-giving showers
Fall all the night on these luminous flowers.

James Clarence Mangan
(1803–1849, Irish poet)

*T*he earth is in love with the heavens, and in the
rainy season the clouds return and fill it with water.

Malik Muhammad Jayasi (writer)

*S*trange what a difference a glorious day can make!
How one revels in life, in being, in poetry, in the holy
ridiculousness of things!

Lionel Johnson
(1867–1902, English critic, poet)

*F*or the man sound in body and serene of mind
there is no such thing as bad weather; every sky has
its beauty, and storms which whip the blood and do
but make it pulse more vigorously.

George Gissing
(1857–1903, English novelist)

*L*ast night, there came a frost, which has done great
damage to my garden . . . It is sad that Nature will
play such tricks with us poor mortals, inviting us with
sunny smiles to confide in her, and then, when we are
entirely within her power, stricking us to the heart.

Nathaniel Hawthorne
(1804–1864, American novelist)

Without the courtyard of the House of State
An orchard of four acres nigh the gate
Is planted with a fence all around it drawn;
And there grow fruit-trees flourishing and great
Pear-laden pomegranates, and apple-trees
Laden with shining apples, and by these,
Sweet-juiced ceases hot nor perishes
Winter or summer, all the year; for there
The western breezes ever soft and fair
Ripen one crop and bring another on.

Homer
(eighth-century B.C. Greek epic poet)

Chapter 6
A Patch of Land

*W*ho loves a garden still his Eden keeps,
Perennial pleasures plants, and wholesome
harvest reaps.

Amos Bronson Alcott, "Tablets"
(1799–1888, American teacher and philosopher)

*O*ur British Gardeners . . . instead of honouring Nature,
love to deviate from it as much as possible. Our trees
rise in Cones, Globes and Pyramids. We see the Marks
of Scissors upon every Plant and Bush . . . For my own
part, I would rather look upon a Tree in all its Luxuri-
ancy and Diffusion of Boughs and Branches than when
it is thus cut and trimmed into a Mathematical Figure.

Andre LeNotre
(French designer)

I just let my brain rest when I paint flowers . . . When
I am painting flowers, I establish the tones, I study the
values carefully, without worrying about losing the
picture. I don't dare to do this with a figure piece for
fear of ruining it. The experience which I gain in these
works I eventually apply to my [figure] pictures.

Pierre-Auguste Renoir,
conversation with Albert Andre,
cited in Albert Andre, Renoir
(French artist)

*E*very landscape is, as it were, a state of the soul, and whoever penetrates into both is astonished to find how much likeness there is in each detail.

Henri Frederic Amiel
(1821–1881, Swiss philosopher and critic)

A knot in the tree spoils the axe; famine spoils friendship.

Anonymous
(Nigeria)

*T*he worship of the trees was apparently among the first forms of religion. The tree of life is found in all of them . . . [trees] became both an object of worth and a feature in gardens, eventually to be elaborated into many magnificent and costly forms.

Richarson Wright,
The Story of Gardening
(1908–1960, magazine editor, garden writer)

*M*oderation is a tree with roots of contentment, and fruits of tranquility and peace.

Anonymous
(Egypt)

*T*he book of life begins with a man and a woman in a garden, and ends with revelations.

Oscar Wilde
(1854–1900, English poet and dramatist)

If you'd have a mind at peace,
A heart that cannot harden—
Go find a door that opens wide
Upon a lovely garden.

Anonymous

The planting of trees is the least self-centered of all that we do. It is a purer act of faith than the procreation of children.

Thornton Wilder
(1897–1975, American playwright)

Some people like to make a little garden out of life and walk down a path.

Jean Anouilh
(1910–1987, French playwright and screenwriter)

Give fools their gold, and knaves their power;
Let fortune's bubbles rise and fall,
Who sows a field, or trains a flower,
Or plants a tree, is more than all.

John Greenleaf Whittier
(1807–1892, American poet)

It all comes back: the odour, grace and hive;
Each sweet relation of its life repeated,
No blank is left, so looking for is cheated.
It is the thing we know.

Mrs. A. D. T. Whitney
(American novelist and poet)

A good book is like a garden carried in the pocket.

Arab proverb

*W*e crowd our blooms and sprays together until they are like the faces of people in the pit of a theater—each lost in the press; a mass, a medley, a tumultary throng. The Japanese treat each gracious beauty of splendour of the garden or the pool as an individual to be honoured, studied, and separately enjoyed.

Sir Edwin Arnold
(1832–1904, English poet and journalist)

A garden that one makes oneself becomes associated with one's personal history and that of one's friends, interwoven with one's tastes, preferences and character, and constitutes a sort of unwritten but withal manifest, autobiography. Show me your garden, provided it be your own, and I will tell you what you are like. It is in middle life that the finishing touches should be put to it; and then, after that, it should remain more or less in the same condition, like oneself, growing more deep of shade, and more protected from the winds . . .

Alfred Austin
(1835–1913, English poet)

I believe a leaf of grass is no less than the journey-work of the stars.

Walt Whitman
(1819–1892, American poet)

You must not know too much, or be too precise or scientific about birds and trees and flowers and watercraft; a certain free margin, and even vagueness—
perhaps ignorance, credulity—helps your enjoyment of these things.

Walt Whitman
(1819–1892, American poet)

God Almighty first planted a garden. And indeed, it is the purest of human pleasures. It is the greatest refreshment to the spirits of man; without which, buildings and palaces are but gross handiworks: and a man shall ever see, that when ages grow to civility and elegancy, men come to build stately, sooner than to garden finally, as if gardening were the greater perfection.

Sir Francis Bacon
(1561–1626, English statesman and writer)

. . . *Like* most people, I wish I could more often be the person I sometimes am—and I am most often that person in the garden.

Lee Bailey, Country Flowers
(cookbook author, home furnishings expert)

A child said, What is the grass? fetching it to me with full hands;
How could I answer the child? I do not know what it is any more than he.

Walt Whitman
(1819–1892, American poet)

$\mathcal{G}$reen are the lawns of country places, and the blooms are abundant. Yet we've wondered often if the dweller in peaceful blooming suburb experiences the grand passions that fires the man with a city back-garden.

E. B. White
(1834–1903, American writer)

$\mathcal{A}$ garden without its statue is like a sentence without a verb.

Joseph W. Beach
(writer)

$\mathcal{I}$t is curious to note how much of love and appreciation certain flowers owe to certain poets. I have a friend who has made a "Shakespeare garden," in which nothing grows which the great magician has not noticed or praised.

Candace Wheeler,
Content in a Garden

$\mathcal{O}$f all formal things in the world, a clipped hedge is the most formal; and of all the informal things in the world, a forest tree is the most informal.

Henry Ward Beecher
(1813–1887, American clergyman and writer)

$\mathcal{T}$he American landscape has no foreground and the American mind has no background.

Edith Wharton
(1861–1937, American novelist)

*N*ature sets her dances to every rhythm, from slow undulations to the swift, dangerous rushes that bring wild exhilaration . . . In the same way a poised mind sweeps out to all new ideas, but is not torn from its place because of its roots.

Mary Webb, 1881–1927,
The Spring of Joy

*O*f all man's works of art, a cathedral is greatest. A vast and majestic tree is greater than that.

Henry Ward Beecher
(1813–1887, American clergyman and writer)

*C*olor, like the fragrance, is intimately connected with light; and between the different rays of the spectrum and the color cells of plants there is a strange telepathy. These processes, so little explored, seem in their deep secrecy and earthly spirituality more marvelous than the most radiant visions of the mystics.

Mary Webb, 1881–1927,
The Spring of Joy

*A*nd gardens with their broad, green walks, where soft the footstep falls.

Henry Glassford Bell,
Mary Queen of Scots
(1803–1874, Scottish author)

They kill good trees to put out bad newspapers.

James G. Watt
(b. 1938, U.S. Secretary of the Interior)

I must go out from this mother of stillness;
I must feel some breath of air
Blowing across cool grass,
and see leaves moving!

Henry Bellaman

I am once more seated under my own vine and fig-tree . . . and hope to spend the remainder of my days . . . which in the ordinary course of things (being now in my sixty-sixth year) cannot be many, in peaceful retirement; making political pursuits yield to the more rational amusement of cultivating the earth.

George Washington,
letter to J. Anderson, April 7, 1797
(1732–1799, American president)

Flowers are love's truest language.

Park Benjamin
(1809–1864, American journalist and verse writer)

Throughout most of history human beings have built their cities with gardens and open spaces . . . our old word "to dwell" fused two older words that had two distinct meanings: to build and to cultivate the land.

Sam Bass Warner, Jr., b. 1928,
To Dwell Is to Garden

*A*vid gardeners and flower arrangers insist that each flower is unique. Allergy sufferers and the florally apathetic remain unimpressed by blossom variety. Both attitudes represent extremes of taste, since "sculpturing" by natural selection has produced a bouquet in which variation sets its own limits.

> *Peter Bernhardt,*
> Wily Violets and Underground Orchids, *1989*
> *(botanist, author, educator)*

*T*he man who has planted a garden feels that he has done something for the good of the whole world.

> *Charles Dudley Warner*
> *(1829–1900, American novelist and essayist)*

*D*o no dishonor to the earth lest you dishonor the spirit of man.

> *Henry Beston*
> *(1888–1968, American writer)*

*N*ature never makes any blunders; when she makes a fool, she means it.

> *Josh Billings*
> *(1818–1885, humorist)*

*T*he world of the gardener and the lover of nature is, in fact, all worlds at all times.

> *Josephine Von Miklos, 1900–1972,*
> The History, the Beauty, the Riches
> of the Gardener's World

*T*o know of someone here and there whom we accord with, who is living on with us, even in silence— This makes our earthly ball a peopled garden.

> *Johann Wolfgang von Goethe*
> *(1749–1831, German writer)*

*I*nstinctively aware of the aesthetic vibrations of plants, which are spiritually satisfying, human beings are happiest and most comfortable when living with flora . . . Our houses are adorned with gardens, our cities with parks, our nations with national preserves.

> *Peter Tomkins and Christopher Bird,*
> The Secret Life of Plants, *1989*

*W*hensoever ye shall plant, it shall be meete and good for you to say as folowith. In the name of God the Father, the Sonne and the Holy Ghost, amen. Increase and Multiplye, and replenish the earth.

> *Unknown,*
> *sixteenth century*

*W*hen California was wild, it was one sweet bee-garden throughout its entire length.

> *John Muir*
> *(1838–1914, American naturalist)*

*I*t has been said that vines are to bits of architecture what a dress is to a woman. It may serve to enhance beauty or to cover defects.

> *Loring Underwood,*
> The Garden & Its Accessories

*A*nd God said, "Behold, I have given you every herb bearing seed which is upon the face of all the earth."

Genesis 1:29

*N*o garden is without its weeds.

Thomas Fuller, M.D.
(1608–1661, English physician, writer)

*E*very artist, scientist, and philosopher in the history of mankind has pointed to the laws of nature as his greatest source of inspiration: without the presence of nature undisturbed, there would have been no Leonardo, no Ruskin, no Nervi, no Frank Lloyd Wright.

Peter Blake, b. 1920,
God's Own Junkyard

*T*he only hunger of our souls is for dreams and flowers.

Paul Jean Toulet
(French poet and novelist)

*L*et a hundred flowers bloom. Let a hundred schools of thought contend.

Mao Tse-tung
(1893–1976, Chinese leader)

The vegetative universe opens like a flower from the earth's center in which is eternity . . .

William Blake
(1757–1827, English poet)

There is just as much beauty visible to us in the landscape as we are prepared to appreciate—not a grain more . . .

Henry David Thoreau
(1817–1862, American naturalist, writer)

Every flower of the field, every fiber of a plant, every particle of an insect, carries with it the impress of its Maker, and can—if duly considered—read us lectures of ethics or divinity.

Sir Thomas Pope Blount
(1618–1679, writer)

When Adam and Eve were dispossessed
Of the garden hard by Heaven,
They planted another down in the west
'Twas Devon, glorious Devon!

Sir Harold Edwin Boulton,
"Glorious Devon" (English poet)

The moon like a flower,
In heaven's high bower,
With silent delight,
Sets and smiles on the night.

William Blake
(1757–1827, English poet)

$\mathscr{C}$ome into the garden, Maude,
For the black bat, night, has flown,
Come into the garden, Maude,
I am here at the gate alone.

Alfred, Lord Tennyson, "Maude"
(1809–1892, English poet)

$\mathscr{G}$od almighty esteemed the life of a man in the garden the happiest he could give him, or else He would not have placed Adam in that of Eden.

Sir William Temple,
Of the Gardens of Epicurus
(1628–1699, English statesman and essayist)

$\mathscr{S}$ympathy with nature is an evidence of perfect health. You cannot perceive beauty but with a serene mind.

Henry David Thoreau
(1817–1862, American naturalist, writer)

$\mathscr{T}$he tree which moves some to tears of joy is in the Eyes of others only a Green thing that stands in the way. Some see Nature all ridicule and deformity, and by these I shall not regulate my proportions; and some scarce see Nature at all. But to the Eyes of the Man of Imagination, Nature is Imagination itself.

William Blake
(1757–1827, English poet)

*W*ilderness is a bench mark, a touchstone. In wilderness we can see where we have come from, where we are going, how far we've gone. In wilderness is the only unsoiled earth sample of forces generally at work in the universe.

Kenneth Bower
(writer)

*G*ardening has been my salvation.

Michael Sylvester
(Wall Street broker)

*W*ithout charm there can be no fine literature,
As there can be no perfect flower without
fragrance.

Arthur Symons
(1865–1945, English journalist and poet)

*H*owever entrancing it is to wander unchecked
through a garden of bright images, are we not entic-
ing your mind from another subject of almost equal
importance?

Ernest Bramah
(English writer)

*F*lowers are the expressions of God's love to man.
One of the highest uses, therefore, which can be made
in contemplating these beautiful creations, in all their
variety and splendor, is, that our thoughts and affections may be drawn upwards to Him who has so
bountifully spread over the face of the whole earth,
such a vast profusion of these beautiful objects, as
tokens of his love to us.

Joseph Breck,
New Book of Flowers

*N*ature never set forth the earth in so rich tapestry
as diverse poets have done, neither with so pleasant
rivers, fruitful trees, sweet-smelling flowers, nor
whatsoever may make the earth more lovely.

Sir Philip Sydney
(1554–1586, writer)

I have loved flowers that fade,
Within whose magic tints
Rich hues have marriage made
With sweet unmemoried scents.

Robert Bridges
(1844–1930,
American poet and editor)

*F*rom place to place had trees the power to move
Nor saw nor axe would wrong the stately grove.

Anwar-I-Suheili
(poet)

*D*esigning a garden, as opposed to just planting it, gives you the power to control the space you have before you.

John Brookes
(English landscape designer)

*O*n each side shrinks the bowery shade,
Before me spreads an emerald glade;
The sunshine steeps its grass and moss,
That couch my footsteps as I cross.

Alfred Street

*T*he materials and plants in a garden and the manner of their disposition are as revealing of its date as are the material and style of a garment, or the wood and detailing of a piece of period furniture.

John Brookes, A Place in the Country
(English garden designer)

The song was written at a time in my life when I was on the road constantly, and what I really needed was to stay home and tend my garden.

Stephen Stills, musician,
on his composition "Johnny's Garden"
(b. 1945, American musician, songwriter)

At the beginning of the twentieth century everything classic equalled symmetry with vistas. Today, there are few vistas. Instead there are car ports (garages) and oil tanks. Pure design terms are very different to other centuries. Today everything is more physical—tennis and basketball courts limit the space in which one has to fit a garden.

John Brookes,
A Place in the Country
(English garden designer)

We travel together, passengers on a little spaceship, dependent on its vulnerable reserves of air and soil, all committed for our safety to its security and peace; preserved from annihilation only by the care, the work, and I will say the love we gave our fragile craft.

Adlai E. Stevenson
(1900–1965, American statesman)

Men but make monuments of sin
Who walk the earth's ambitious round;
Thou hast the richer realm within
This garden ground.

Alice Brown
(1856–1948, American poet and novelist)

$\mathcal{N}$ot God! in Gardens! When the eve is cool?
Nay, but I have a sign:
'Tis very sure God walks in mine.

> *Thomas Edward Brown*
> *(1830–1897, British poet)*

$\mathcal{W}$e tend to clutter gardens without considering the
style of it.

> *John Brookes,*
> *A Place in the Country*
> *(English garden designer)*

$\mathcal{T}$hou that dwellest in the gardens . . .
Cause me to hear thy voice Anon.

> *Song of Solomon 8:13*

$\mathcal{A}$ll that in this delightful garden grows,
Should happy be, and have immortal Bliss.

> *Edmund Spenser,*
> *"The Shepherd's Calendar"*
> *(1552–1599, English poet)*

$\mathcal{A}$ll things are artificial, for nature is the art of God.

> *Sir Thomas Browne*
> *(1605–1682, English writer and scholar)*

These are the gardens of the desert, these
The unshorn fields, boundless and beautiful,
For which the speech of England has no name—
The prairies.

William Cullen Bryant
(1794–1878, American poet)

An early worshipper at Nature's shrine,
I loved her rudest scenes—warrens, and heaths
And yellow commons, and birch-shaded hollows,
And hedgerows bordering unfrequented lanes,
Bowered with wild roses and the clasping woodbine.

Charlotte Smith
(English writer)

As I have gardened, feeling myself in some sort of
deep dialogue with an unseen and silent partner, I
have come to know true inner peace.

Martha Smith,
Beds I Have Known, *1990*

This mighty oak—
By whose immovable stem I stand and seem
        almost annihilated—not a prince
In all that proud old world beyond the deep
E'er wore his crown as loftily as he wears the
        green corona of leaves with which
Thy hand has graced him.

William Cullen Bryant
(1794–1878, American poet)

My tent stands in a garden
Of aster and golden-rod
Filled by the rain and sunshine,
And sown by the hand of God.

William Bliss Carman,
An Autumn Garden
(1861–1929, American poet)

Is the fancy too far brought, that this love for gardens
is a reminiscence haunting the race of that remote time
when but two persons existed—a gardener named
Adam, and a gardener's wife called Eve?

Alexander Smith
(1830–1867, Scottish writer)

There is virtue in the open, there is healing
out of doors;
The great physician makes his rounds along
the forest floors.
Have little care that life is brief, and less
that art is long.
Success is in the silences
Though fame is in the song.

William Bliss Carman
(1861–1929, American poet)

The pursuit of happiness is a planet whose resources
are devoted to the physical and spiritual nourishment
of its inhabitants.

Jimmy Carter
(b. 1924, American president, politician, humanitarian)

*H*ere sea laps earth's foundation, here is seen
the weltering ground with Ocean's
foliage green;
Lo, sea-flower gardens, land and deep combined,
And Naiad springs with Nereid flood entwined.

Paulus Silentarus
(Greek poet)

*T*hat nature is out of date suggests that what we think of as a love of nature is a kind of fashionable sentiment. The difficulty is that this is both true and false. It is a sea of feelings, psychic imagery, literary and poetic insight, economic heritage, perceptual habit, and other factors interwoven with their own public and distorted manifestations. Nature is real and love of nature is part of reality.

Paul Shepard,
Man in the Landscape

I like trees because them seem more resigned to the way they have to live than other things do.

Willa Cather,
O Pioneers!
(1873–1947, writer, poet)

*A*rt is the unceasing effort to compete with the beauty of flowers—and never succeeding.

Marc Chagall
(1887–1985, French artist)

$\mathscr{E}$xcept during the nine months before he draws his first breath, no man manages his affairs as well as a tree does.

George Bernard Shaw
(1856–1950, British dramatist, novelist, critic)

$\mathscr{O}$ur bodies are our gardens, to the which our wills are gardeners.

William Shakespeare,
Othello
(English dramatist and poet)

$\mathscr{T}$his garden full of leaves and flowers;
And craft of man's hand so curiously
Arrayed had this garden, truly
That never was there garden of such prys
But if it were the very paradise.

Geoffrey Chaucer,
The Franklin's Tale
(c. 1342–1400, English poet)

$\mathscr{T}$here is hardly any such thing in Nature as a mere droop of weakness. Rigidity yielding a little, like justice swayed by mercy, is the whole beauty of the earth.

G. K. Chesterton
(1874–1936, English essayist, novelist, and poet)

*M*an has been so noisy about the way he has "conquered nature," and Nature has been so silent in her persistent influence over man, that the geographic factor in the equation of human development has been overlooked.

> *Ellen Semple,*
> Influences of Geographic Environment
> on the Basis of Ratzel's System
> of Anthropology-Geography
> *(scientist)*

*T*he Earth that's nature's mother is her tomb, what is her burying grave that is her womb, and from her womb children of divers kind we sucking on her natural bosom find, many for the virtues excellent none but for some and yet all different. O mickle is the powerful grace that lies in plants, herbs, stones and their true qualities, for naught so vile that on the earth doth live but to the earth some special good doth give.

> *William Shakespeare,*
> Romeo and Juliet
> *(1564–1616, English dramatist and poet)*

*W*eary travelers, journeying west,
In the shade of the trees find pleasant rest;
And often they start with glad surprise,
At the rosy fruit that round them lies.

> *Lydia Maria Child*
> *(b. 1912, American writer)*

A stone hewn into a gracefully ornamented vase or urn has a value which it did not before possess; a yew hedge clipped into a fortification is only defaced. The one is a product of art, the other a distortion of nature.

Sir Walter Scott
(1771–1832, Scottish novelist and poet)

*I*t is a consoling thought that gardens and their laws of birth and death endure, while political crises and panaceas appear only to vanish.

Vida P. Scudder
(writer)

*H*e has so enveloped everything with ivy, not only the foundation walls of the villa, but also the spaces between the columns of the promenade, that I declare the Greek statues seem to be in business as landscape gardeners, and to be advertising their ivy.

Cicero, writing of his brother's topiaries
in Epistulae ad Quintum Fratrem
(106–43 B.C., Latin philosopher and statesman)

*I*n the lower part of the garden there are high trees, and, amongst there, the tulip tree and the live oak. Beyond the garden is a large clump of lofty sycamores, and, in these a most populous rookery, in which, all things in the world I delight.

William Cobbett
(1763–1835, writer, editor, politician)

*I*nto any garden, no matter how artificial or how tame, some wild things will find their way. It is a shallow boast, this talk that we hear about man's conquest of nature.

Herbert Ravenel Sass,
Adventures in Green Places

*I*n the end, there is really nothing more important than taking care of the earth and letting it take care of you.

Charles Scott
(president, National Gardening Association)

We do not inherit the land from our ancestors; we borrow it from our children.

Native American saying

The flower, if standing by itself, would be no great beauty; but, contrasted thus, with the fresh grass, which was a little shorter than itself, it was very beautiful.

William Cobbett
(1763–1835, writer, editor, politician)

There's something in a noble tree—
What shall I say? a soul?
For 'tis not form, or aught we see
In leaf or branch or bole.
Some presence, though not understood,
Dwells there away, and seems
To be acquainted with our mood,
And mingles in our dreams.

Samuel Valentine Cole
(American poet)

Is there a joy except gardening that asks so much, and gives so much? I know of no other except, perhaps the writing of a poem. They are much alike, even in the amount of waste that has to be accepted for the sake of the rare, chancy joy when all goes well.

May Sarton, 1912–1985,
Plant Dreaming Deep

$\mathcal{W}$e are still in Eden; the wall that shuts us out of the garden is our own ignorance and folly.

Thomas Cole
(1801–1848, English writer)

$\mathcal{T}$he Admiral says that he never beheld so fair a thing: Trees all along the river, beautiful and green, and different from ours, with flowers and fruits each according to their kind, many birds and little birds which sing very sweetly.

Christopher Columbus
(1451–1506 explorer)

$\mathcal{I}$t is closing time in the gardens of the west and from now on an artist will be judged only by the resonance of his solitude or the quality of his despair.

Cyril Connolly
(1903–1974, English essayist, novelist, critic)

$\mathcal{R}$epetition is the only form of permanence that nature can achieve.

George Santayana
(1863–1952, Spanish-born writer and essayist)

$\mathcal{A}$rt is nature as seen through a temperament.

Jean-Baptiste-Camille Corot
(1796–1875, artist)

A gardener is never rich, yet he is ever raking together. His knowledge consists in the vegetative knowledge of plants. Like Adam, he is put into some gentleman's garden to dress the trees, and to make it if he can, a Paradise of Pleasure, and for this he has his yearly wages.

Wye Saltonstall,
"Pictures Drawn Forth in Characters"

We cannot fathom the mystery of a single flower, nor is it intended that we should; but that the pursuit of science should constantly be betrayed by the love of beauty, and accuracy of knowledge by tenderness of emotion.

John Ruskin
(1819–1900, English critic, artist,
and social reformer)

My garden all is overblown with roses,
My spirit all is overblown with rhyme . . .

Vita Sackville-West
(1892–1962, British poet and novelist)

A plow on a field arable is the most honorable of ancient arms.

Abraham Cowley
(1618–1667, English poet)

*T*hat spiritual garden accompanies them
        everywhere
Yet is never revealed to the eyes of the people,
Its fruits ever asking to be gathered,
Its fount of life welling up to be drunk.

Jalaluddin Rumi
(thirteenth-century Persian philosopher and poet)

*O*the green things growing, the green
        things growing,
The faint smell of the green things growing.

Dinah Maria Mulock Craik,
"The Green Things Growing"
(1826–1887, writer, poet)

*T*hus it is that a garden gradually becomes a repository
of human emotions. As we draw from it our comfort, so
does it draw from us inward and outward character.

Agnes Rothery
(writer)

*O*nly a few Human beings should grow to tree square
mill. They commonly are planted too close.

William T. Dairs
(writer)

There is a concept I love to contemplate because it is simple, beautiful and true: that growing, harvesting, preparing, presenting, and eating foods from the garden are all phases of the same activity. Each step is part of the satisfying process of partaking of the earth's bounty.

Rosalind Creasy,
Cooking from the Garden, *1988*
(cookbook writer)

It is nice to be a flower; but it is perhaps nicer to be a man, if one can.

Romain Rolland
(1866–1944, French essayist, novelist, biographer)

What then I say is this, that we ignoramuses who know very little about it can derive a pure pleasure, not merely from the contemplations of gardens, but from the reading of books about them.

Archibald Philip Primrose, Earl of Rosebury
(English foreign secretary and prime minister)

Though truly determined lovers will meet almost anywhere, the garden is their natural trysting place, just as it was for Romeo and Juliet, Pyramus and Thisbe, Adam and Eve.

Barbara Damrosch,
Theme Gardens
(American landscape designer, author)

$\mathcal{I}$ know a man who is a poet. It is true that he would not know himself by such a title, for he does not write a verse; he is a farmer. He is a poet because he knows the joy of creation. A never-failing delight in the appearance of living, growing plants in a patch of dirt where, a few days before, he has placed some dry grains.

Harold William Rickett,
The Green Earth
(b. 1896, staff member, New York Botanical Garden)

$\mathcal{T}$ here are places in the heart which might have been gardens, or favorite quarter, around which we have built high walls, whose doors have been shut too long.

Guy Davenport,
"Apples and Pears"
(b. 1927, writer)

$\mathcal{I}$ f you've seen one redwood tree, you've seen 'em all.

Ronald Reagan
(b. 1911, American president and actor)

$\mathcal{S}$ hall I ever play again in my mother's garden-close?

Marceline Desbordes-Valmore
(French actress, poet)

The greatest domestic problem facing our country is saving our soil and water. Our soil belongs also to unborn generations.

Sam Rayburn, quoted by Valton J. Young
(1882–1961, U.S. politician)

Garden of garden born
Through centuries,
Eve may have gathered flowers
Like some of these.

Louise Driscoll
(American poet and writer)

It is only at the tree loaded with fruit that the people throw stones.

French proverb

Patience is a flower that grows not in everyone's garden.

John Ray
(1627–1705, English naturalist
and collector of proverbs)

Anyone who has got any pleasure at all from nature should try to put something back. Life is like a superlative meal and the world is the maître d'hôtel. What I am doing is the equivalent of leaving a reasonable tip.

Gerald Durrell
(b. 1925, writer)

$\mathcal{W}$ho really cares from where our zest for gardens originates? Whether from myth, hearsay or historical facts, from paradise or Persia, let's be less cerebral and more electically wanton. Merely thinking formless thoughts is enough to add another thrust to the whole gardening mystique.

Mirabel Osler,
A Gentle Plea for Chaos,
The Enchantment of Gardening
(author, garden writer)

$\mathcal{W}$here'er you walk, cool gales shall fan the glade,
Trees, where you sit, shall crowd into a shade:
Where'er you tread, the blushing flow'rs shall rise,
And all things flourish where you turn your eyes.

Alexander Pope
(1688–1744, English poet and critic)

$\mathcal{I}$t has always seemed to me that the punishment of the first gardener and his wife was the bitterest of all. To have lived always in a garden "where grew every tree pleasant to the sight and good for food," to have known no other place, and then to have been driven forth into the great world without hope of returning! Oh! Ever had you not desired wisdom, your happy children might still be tilling the soil of that blessed Eden.

Helena Rutherfurd Ely,
A Woman's Hardy Garden

223

I've often wished that I had clear,
For life, six hundred pounds a year,
A handsome house to lodge a friend,
A river at my garden's end,
A terrace walk, and half a rood
Of land set out to plant a wood.

Alexander Pope
(1688–1744, English poet and critic)

*L*ove of flowers and all things green and growing is with many men and women a passion so strong that it often seems to be sort of a primal instinct, coming down through generation after generation, from the first man who was put into a garden "to dress it and to keep it."

Helena Rutherfurd Ely,
A Woman's Hardy Garden

*S*cience cannot solve the ultimate mystery of nature. And that is because, in the last analysis, we ourselves are part of nature and therefore part of the mystery that we are trying to solve.

Max Planck
(1858–1947, German physicist)

A tree in its old age is like a bent but mellowed and wise old man; it inspires our respect and tender admiration; it is too noble to need our pity.

Donald Culross Peattie,
An Almanac for Moderns
(1898–1964, American botanist)

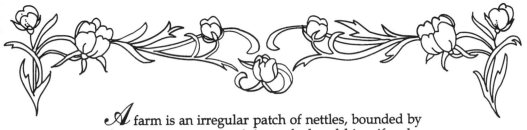

A farm is an irregular patch of nettles, bounded by short-term notes, containing a fool and his wife who didn't know enough to stay in the city.

S. J. Perelman
(1904–1979, American humorist)

*I*f I could put my woods in song
And tell what's there enjoyed,
All men would to my gardens throng,
And leave the cities void.

Ralph Waldo Emerson
(1803–1882, American writer)

*R*emember, this planet is also disposable.

Paul Palmer
(writer)

*G*ardens, ponds, palings, the creation, roamed with the purity of tears, are only categories of passion, hoarded by the human heart.

Boris Pasternak,
"Definition of the Creative Power"
(1890–1960, Russian Jewish poet and novelist)

*T*he first farmer was the first man; all historic nobility rests on the possession and use of land.

Ralph Waldo Emerson
(1803–1882, American writer)

*T*here's nothing like waving hollyhock to make you into an action painter!

Mary Page Evans
(writer)

*T*hough we travel the world over to find beauty, we must carry it with us or we find it not . . .

Ralph Waldo Emerson
(1803–1882, American writer)

*I*t is only to the gardener that time is a friend, giving each year more than he steals.

Beverly Nichols,
from "Merry Hall"
(1898–1983, British writer)

*S*ilent flowers
speak also
to that obedient ear within.

Haiku by Onitsura
(Oriental poet)

*W*ho dares to say that trees and plants have no soul? The truth is that I have seen many laugh and many cry.

Louis Notari
(Monegasque poet)

*W*ho leaves the pine-tree, leaves his friend,
Unnerves his strength, invites his end.

Ralph Waldo Emerson
(1803–1882, American writer)

I love people to a certain extent, but sometimes I want to get off in the garden to talk with God. I have the blooms, and when the blooms are gone, I love to watch the green. God dressed the world in green.

Minnie Evans
(writer)

The moon of my delight who know'st no wane,
The moon of heav'n is rising once again:
How oft hereafter rising shall she look
Through this same Garden after me—in vain!

Edward Fitzgerald
(1809–1883, English poet and translator)

I think that I shall never see
A billboard lovely as a tree,
Perhaps, unless the billboards fall,
I'll never see a tree at all.

Ogden Nash
(1902–1971, American humorist)

By a garden is meant mystically a place of spiritual repose, stillness, peace, refreshment, delight.

Cardinal John Henry Newman
(1801–1890, religious leader, Catholic prelate)

Man's spirit cannot be shut off from nature and from beauty unless civilization is prepared to pay a better price . . . the worth of beauty is greater than the passing pleasure it affords.

Orville L. Freeman
(American politician)

*T*he body politic is like a tree; as it proceeds upwards, it stands as much in need of heaven as of earth.

Honoré Gabriel, Comte de Mirabeau
(statesman)

*A*ncient Hebrew law forbade the destruction of trees even when sacking a city.

Barbara Gallup and Deborah Reich,
The Complete Book of Totally Topiary
(horticulturists and writers)

*O*ur national flower is the concrete cloverleaf.

Lewis Mumford
(1895–1990, American writer)

. . . *W*hen the divine balanced beauty of the trees and flowers seemed to be reflected and doubled by all the onlooking rocks and streams as though they were mirrors, while they in turn were mirrored in every garden and grove.

John Muir,
South of Yosemite
(1838–1914, American naturalist)

229

$\mathscr{B}$uddha saw the light while sitting under a tree; therefore trees were associated with him and many of his followers believed trees had souls.

Barbara Gallup and Deborah Reich,
The Complete Book of
Totally Topiary, *1988*
(horticulturists and writers)

(For some days, people thought that India was shaking.)

$\mathscr{B}$ut there are always tremors when a great tree falls.

Rajiv Gandhi
(b. 1944, Indian statesman)

$\mathscr{O}$ther holidays repose in the past; Arbor Day proposes for the future.

Sterling Morton,
from Flower & Garden Magazine,
March/April 1990
(1832–1902, garden writer)

$\mathscr{I}$ shall make my garden
As true men build a shrine.

Theodosia Garrison
(American poet)

230

*I*n this pleasant soil
His far more pleasant garden God ordained.
Out of the fertile ground he caused to grow.
And trees of noblest kind for sight, smell, taste;
And amid all them stood the Tree of Life.

John Milton
(1608–1674, English epic poet)

*A*nd add to these retired leisure,
That in trim gardens takes his pleasure.

John Milton
(1608–1674, English epic poet)

*I*f thou sit here to new this pleasant
        garden place,
Think thus: at last will come a frost and all
        these flowers deface:
But if thou sit at ease to rest thy weary bones,
Remember death brings final rest of all our
        grievous groans;
So whether for delight, or here thou sit for ease,
Think still upon the latter day: so shall thou
        God best please.

George Gascoigne
(1525–1577, English poet)

*A*ll lovers' ghosts to gardens come again,
Seeking remembered Edens with an art
Indelible as music in the heart.

Ernest Hartsock (poet)

$\mathscr{G}$ardening has compensations out of all proportions to its goals. It is creation in the pure sense.

Phyllis McGinley
(writer)

$\mathscr{A}$ cynic is a man who, when he smells flowers, looks around for a coffin.

H. L. Mencken
(1880–1956, American editor, satirist, writer)

$\mathscr{G}$ive me the clear blue sky over my head, and green turf beneath my feet, a winding road before me.

W. Hazlitt, 1778–1830,
Flower & Gardening Magazine,
October/November 1991

$\mathscr{T}$o dwell is to garden.

Martin Heidegger
(1889–1976, writer)

$\mathscr{H}$ow could such sweet and wholesome hours Be reckoned but with herbs and flowers?

Andrew Marvell
(1621–1678, English poet and satirist)

*L*ove your neighbor, yet pull not down your hedge.

George Herbert
(1593–1633, English poet)

*Y*ou have now discovered the truth about yourself. Your parents gave you a great start. You were planted in good soil—fed—watered—carefully nurtured . . . But have you accomplished all that you could have—given your beginning? . . . It's a bit late now, but profit by this—if you do it—do it. Get those weeds out. And plant carefully.

Katharine Hepburn,
Me
(b. 1909, American actress)

*F*air Quiet, have I found thee here,
And Innocence, thy sister dear?
Mistake long, I sought you then
In busy companies of men.
Your sacred plants, if here below,
Only among the plants will grow;
Society is all but rude
To this delicious solitude.

Andrew Marvell
(1621–1678, English poet and satirist)

*I*got me flowers to strew the way,
I got me boughs off many a tree: But
thou was up by break of day,
And brought'st thy sweets
along with thee.

George Herbert
(1593–1633, English poet)

*A*nnihilating all that's made
To a green thought in a green shade.

Andrew Marvell
(1621–1678, English poet, satirist)

*F*riend, walk thine own dear
garden grounds,
Not enjoying others' larger bounds;
For well thou know'st 'tis not extent
Makes happiness, but sweet content.

Robert Herrick
(1591–1674, English poet)

*L*awn: A place where hardy grasses, that flourish in
empty lots and grow between the cracks in sidewalks,
wither and die from the householder's tender care.

Burton Hillis,
as quoted in Reader's Digest,
June 1955

This is a darling little garden when one can get out of one's shell and look at it. But what does it profit a man to look at anything if he is not free? Unless one is free to offer oneself up wholely and solely to the pansy—one receives nothing. It's promiscuous love instead of a living relationship—a dead thing.

Katherine Mansfield
(1888–1923, author)

The roses: their richness, variety, etc., will no doubt always make them necessary to the poets.

Gerard Manley Hopkins
(1844–1889, poet)

Happy the man who, far away from business Cares, like the pristine race of mortals, works his ancestral acres with his steers.

Horace
(65–8 B. C. Latin poet)

Where would we be if humanity had never known flowers? If they didn't exist and had always been hidden from view . . . our characters, our morals, our aptitude for beauty, for happiness, would they be the same?

Maurice Maeterlinck

$\mathcal{T}$he child of civilization, remote from wild nature and her ways, is more susceptible to her grandeur than is her untutored son who has looked at her and lived close to her from childhood up, on terms of prosaic familiarity.

Thomas Mann
(1875–1955, German novelist and essayist)

$\mathcal{S}$oil fertility is the basis of the public health system of the future.

Sir Albert Howard
(statesman)

$\mathcal{T}$he pine is the mother of legends.

James Russell Lowell
(1819–1891, American poet and critic)

$\mathcal{B}$eneath some patriarchal tree
I lay upon the ground;
His hoary arms uplifted he,
And all the broad leaves over me
Clapped their little hands in glee,
with one continuous sound.

Henry Wadsworth Longfellow
(1807–1882,
American poet and scholar)

*T*he human race has a desire—as powerful in the aboriginal as it is in the twentieth century . . . not to leave well enough alone but to add decoration; and the meaning of the verb "to decorate" is to "adorn or beautify."

Peter Hunt,
The Book of Garden Ornament

*W*hether we look, or whether we listen
We hear life murmur, or see it glisten;
Every clod feels a stir of might,
An instinct within it that reaches and towers,
And, groping blindly above it for light,
Climbs to a soul in grass and flowers.

James Russell Lowell
(1874–1925, American poet and critic)

*E*very part of the ecosystem on earth depends on the green life-support apparatus for its survival as a whole.

Anthony Huxley,
Green Inheritance
(botanist, conservationist, author)

*P*opulation [will] increase rapidly, more rapidly than in former times and ere long the most valuable of all arts will be the art of deriving a comfortable subsistence from the smallest area of soil.

Abraham Lincoln
(1809–1865, American president)

How many, many days have I explored
The grove; and flower on flower, herb on herb,
Scented and tasted! Yea, without reward—
My heart a burden that my pains perturb,
My step a draggled vagabond,—to rove
Through time turned centuries, and worlds
        a grove!

Juana Ines de la Cruz
(Spanish poet)

If a tree dies, plant another in its place.

Carl Linnaeus
(1707–1778, Swedish botanist)

Trees will come down to the shore of a lake and
grow there, and sometimes they will lean out over the
water. It was that way that I first discovered that trees
are vain. It was them standing by the hour looking at
themselves. A lake is the vanity case of the tree.

Thomas Jefferson
(1743–1826, American president)

The danger of exposing ourselves to any art—
including gardens—is that we see only details, limit
ourselves to labels and fail to comprehend the sum
and substance of what the artist has said.

Carlton B. Lees,
Gardens, Plants & Man
(b. 1924, executive director of
Massachusetts Horticultural Society,
landscape designer, photographer)

*C*onservation is a state of harmony between men and land.

Aldo Leopold
(1886–1948, American forester and conservationist)

*U*nder cherry-flowers
None are strangers.

Issa,
from Haiku Poems,
Ancient & Modern
(Oriental poet)

*A*s cities sprawl across the land, the opportunities to experience natural landscape become fewer and fewer. Since man's very existence depends upon plants, it is essential that he have contact with them in order to recognize himself in the total scheme of things.

Carlton B. Lees,
Gardens, Plants & Man
(b. 1924, executive director of
Massachusetts Horticultural Society,
landscape designer, photographer)

A farm, however large, is not more difficult to direct than a garden, and does not call for more attention or skill.

Thomas Jefferson
(1743–1826, American president)

239

$\mathcal{T}$he earth belongs always to the living generation: they may manage it, then and what proceeds from it, as they please, during their usufruct.

Thomas Jefferson
(1743–1826, American president)

$\mathcal{I}$ knew just what I needed: ferns, ferns and hostas go together like bacon and eggs, or the bass Samuel Ramey and operas by Handel.

Allen Lacy
(American garden writer)

$\mathcal{T}$here is not a sprig of grass that shoots uninteresting to me, nor anything that moves.

Thomas Jefferson
(1743–1826, American president)

$\mathcal{S}$mall gardens filled with amorous blossoms where felonious darts of love spring through the air.

Louise Labe
(French poet, linguist, feminist)

$\mathcal{P}$erhaps the chief charm of the herbalist is just that they are more likely than the modern scientist to impart a sense and wonder—both of which the scientist may feel, but considers it no part of his function to communicate.

Joseph Wood Krutch, Herbal
(1893–1970, American naturalist)

*J*ust as an unassorted assemblage of mere words, though they may be the best words in our language, will express no thought, or as the purest colours on an artist's palette—so long as they remain on the palette—do not form a picture, so our garden plants, placed without due consideration or definite intention, cannot show what they can best do for us.

> *Gertrude Jekyll,*
> *"A Definite Purpose in Gardening"*
> *(English garden writer)*

O for a lodge in a garden of cucumbers!
O for an iceberg or two at control!
O for a vale which at midday the dew cumbers!
O for a pleasure trip to the Pole!

> *Rossiter Johnson,*
> *"Ninety-Nine in the Shade"*
> *(American author)*

*P*ersonally, I feel both happier and more secure when I am reminded that I have the backing of something older and perhaps more permanent than I am— the something I mean, which taught the flower to count to five and the beetle to know that spots are more pleasing if arranged in a definite order. Some of the most important secrets are, they assure me, known to others than myself.

> *Joseph Wood Krutch,*
> The Best of Two Worlds
> *(1893–1970, American naturalist)*

The garden is very handsomely laid out in squares and flower knots and contains a great variety of trees, flowers and plants of foreign growth collected from every part of the world.

Reverend John E. Latta
(clergyman)

A cow is a very good animal in the field; but we turn her out of a garden.

Samuel Johnson in a letter to Lord Chesterfield
(1709–1784, English lexicographer, essayist, poet)

Scents are the soul of flowers: they may even be perceptible in the land of shadows.

Joseph Joubert
(1754–1824, French moralist and essayist)

It was at the charming, vine-covered cottage in Argenteuil that Monet created his first garden, reflecting his lifelong delight in flowers.

Claire Joyes,
Monet's Table, *1990*
(Monet authority)

The desire to impose man's will on nature lies behind all the gardens that have been created over the past 3,000 years.

Libraire Larousse,
Gardening & Gardens

*T*all oaks, branch-charmed by the earnest stars,
Dream and so dream all night without a stir.

John Keats
(1795–1821, English poet)

*I*t is our task in our time and in our generation to
hand down undiminished to those who come after us,
as was handed down to us by those who went before,
the natural wealth and beauty which is ours.

John F. Kennedy
(1917–1963, American president)

*C*anst thou prophecy, thou little tree,
What the glory of thy boughs shall be?

Lucy Larcom
(American editor and poet)

*I*t is for each gardener to define his own objectives,
his own ideal, so the garden becomes a natural extension of the gardener's personality.

Libraire Larousse,
Gardening & Gardens

*T*he odors of fruits waft me to my southern home, to
my childhood frolics in the peach orchard.

Helen Keller,
"A Natural History of the Senses"
(1880–1968, American writer and educator)

243

*E*ven the general
　　Took off his armor
　　　to gaze
　　At our peonies.

Kikaku,
from Haiku Harvest, 1989
(Oriental poet)

A little thin, flowery border, neat, not gaudy.

Charles Lamb
(1775–1834, English writer)

*H*e who plants a tree plants hope.

Lucy Larcom
(American editor and poet)

*A*nd the sun shone and the cuckoo called and the pear tree waved his blossoms, and all the sweet flower scents went up in fragrant incense and praise to God, and I gathered cowslip and bluebells and was happy as a child.

Francis Kilvert
(1840–1879, clergyman)

*T*he love of flowers brings surely with it the love of all the green world.

Mrs. Francis King,
The Well-Considered Garden

$\mathcal{E}$verything in the universe has a purpose, and that purpose is God's glory, man's welfare, or usually, both.

Joseph Wood Krutch, Herbal
(1893–1970, American naturalist)

$\mathcal{I}$f my eye lights upon the carefully tended peony held up by a barrel hoop, the round group of an old dicentra, the fine upstanding single plant of iris, at once I experience the warmest feeling of friendliness for that householder, and wish to know and talk with them about their flowers. For at the bottom there is a bond which breaks down every other difference between us. We are "garden souls."

Mrs. Francis King,
The Well-Considered Garden

$\mathcal{O}$ur England is a garden that is full of stately views,
Of borders, beds and shrubberies and lawns
    and avenues,
With statues on the terraces and peacocks strutting by;
but the Glory of the Garden lies in more than meets
    the eye.

Rudyard Kipling,
"The Glory of the Garden"
(1865–1936, English writer)

Chapter 7
It Begins with a Seed

Roses are red, violets are blue;
But they don't get around like the
dandelions do.

Slim Acres
(American poet)

Pluck not the wayward flower;
It is the traveler's dower.

William Allingham
(1824–1889, English poet)

Amid a host of alien weeds
Spring faces of familiar blooms
Which, breathing stories in perfumes,
See ghosts of some forgotten seeds.

Frank Dempster Sherman
(American poet)

(On strawberries:)

Doubtless God could have made a better berry, but
doubtless God never did.

Dr. William Butler, 1535–1618

When I was a boy I thought scent was contained in the dewdrops on flowers and if I got up very early in the morning, I could collect it and make perfume. To my great disappointment it was not there at all.

Oscar de la Renta,
from House & Garden *magazine, April 1992*
(b. 1932, fashion designer)

Let Patience grow in your garden.

Anonymous

You must grow like a tree, not like a mushroom.

Janet Erskine Stuart
(writer)

He who plants pears
Plants fruit for his heirs.

Anonymous

Though I do not believe that a plant will spring up where no seed has been, I have great faith in a seed . . . Convince me that you have a seed there, and I am prepared to expect wonders. I shall even believe that the millennium is at hand.

Henry David Thoreau
(1817–1862, American naturalist, writer)

The split tree still grows.

Anonymous (Senegal/Gambia)

*M*ystery glows in the rose bed,
The secret is hidden in the rose.

Farīdod-Dīn Attār
(Persian poet)

*A*nd I will make thee beds of roses
And a thousand fragrant posies.

Christopher Marlowe,
"The Passionate Shepherd To His Love"
(1564–1593, English dramatist)

*O*bvious though our dependence upon plants may
be, we have, it seems taken it for granted that they
will continue to exist in all their variety no matter
how we treat them and the land on which they grow.

David Attenborough
(b. 1926, author, naturalist)

*U*nkempt about those hedges blows
An unofficial English rose.

Rupert Brooke,
"The Old Vicarage, Grantchester"
(1887–1915, British poet)

*A*nd because the breath of flowers is far sweeter in
the aire than in the hand, therefore nothing is more fit
for that delight than to know what be the flowers and
plants that doe best perfume the aire.

Sir Francis Bacon
(1561–1626, English statesman, writer)

O mickle is the powerful grace that lies in herbs, plants, stones and their true qualities.

William Shakespeare,
Romeo and Juliet
(1564–1616 English dramatist, poet)

*J*ust now the lilac is in bloom
All before my little room.

Rupert Brooke,
"The Old Vicarage, Grantchester"
(1887–1915, English poet)

*H*orticulture is concerned with the cultivation of plants. The plant is the beginning and the end. For the plant we till the soil, build greenhouses, and transact the business of the garden.

Liberty Hyde Bailey,
The Survival of the Unlike
(1858–1954, horticulturist)

*F*lowers . . . have a mysterious and subtle influence upon the feelings, not unlike some strains of music. They relax the tenseness of the mind. They dissolve its rigor.

Henry Ward Beecher
(1813–1887, American clergyman, writer)

*A*nything green that grew out of the mould
Was an excellent herb to our fathers of old.

Rudyard Kipling, 1865–1936,
"Grandmother's Secrets"

I have loved flowers that fade,
Within whose magic tents
Rich hues have marriage made
With sweet unmemoried scents.

Robert Bridges, 1844–1930,
from Shorter Poems, Book II

*F*lowers are the sweetest things God ever made and forgot to put a soul into.

Henry Ward Beecher
(1813–1887, American clergyman, writer)

*T*he cultivation of choice fruit had a tendency to promote the health and happiness of a family; affording a greater luxury, and a better, than the imported fruits.

Farmer's Almanac, 1846

*Y*ou cannot forget if you would those golden kisses all over the cheeks of the meadow, queerly called "dandelions."

Henry Ward Beecher
(1813–1887, American clergyman, writer)

*O*ne of the healthiest ways to gamble is with a spade and a package of garden seeds.

Dan Bennett
(writer)

*H*erimone. But, ah! so fleetingly do their
　　　lives pass.
That even when their bloom the richest glows.
I, looking forward to its swift decay,
Feel a strange sadness as I gaze on them and
　　　thoughts of death come o'er me.

Marguerite Blessington
(countess, English novelist)

*S*catter ye seeds each passing year,
Sow amid winds and storms of rain,
Hope give the courage,
Faith cast out fear,
God will requite thee
With infinite grain.

Farmer's Almanac, 1854

I like to see flowers growing, but when they are
gathered they cease to please. I never offer flowers to
those I love; I never wish to receive them from hands
dear to me.

Charlotte Brontë
(1816–1855, English novelist, poet)

(On spring:)

. . . *A*nd out in the vegetable garden the asparagus
jumped six inches, I swear. There wasn't a stalk worth
picking in sight this morning, and by late afternoon
we found all we could eat for supper, up and ready
for cutting.

Hal Borland, 1900–1978,
Hal Borland's Book of Days

(On strawberries:)

*T*his delicious fruit is so easily cultivated, so health-ful, and so universally popular, that it is worthwhile for every farmer to raise it in quantities sufficient, at least to supply his own family. Indeed why should not all the small fruits receive greater attention in every farmer's garden? They ripen for the most part at the season of the year when other fruits are scarce, and their free use is unquestionably conducive to health.

Farmer's Almanac, 1872

*H*e places a seed in the dust for a reason
That it may in the day of distress, give fruit.

Sadi
(1213–1292, Persian poet)

*M*any flowers present strong distinctive characters, or will, at least often do, excite in us variable feelings: the primrose, and the daisy, if not intrinsically gay, call forth cheerful and pleasing sensations: and the aspect or glance of some others will awaken different affections.

John Leonard Knapp
(soldier, illustrator, writer)

*N*ever plant in the garden all at one time, but begin as early as the land is in good condition, and plant something every week until August.

Farmer's Almanac, 1887

$\mathscr{W}$ho, that was blessed with parents that indulged themselves, and children with a flower garden, can forget the happy innocent hours spent in its cultivation! O! who can forget those days, when to announce the appearance of a bud, or the coloring of a tulip, or the opening of a rose, or the perfection of a full-blown peony, was glory enough for one morning.

Joseph Breck, New Book of Flowers

$\mathscr{T}$he ivy is a dependant plant, and delights in waste and ruin. We do not often tolerate its growth when the building is in repair and perfect; but if time dilapidates the edifice, the ivy takes possession of the fragment, and we call it beautiful.

John Leonard Knapp
(soldier, illustrator, writer)

*I*n my opinion, the man who conveys, and causes to grow, in any country a grain, a fruit, or even a flower, it never possessed before, deserves more praise than a thousand heroes: he is a benefactor, he is in some degree a creator.

Frances Brooke
(English author, editor)

*A*ny nose
May ravage with impunity the rose.

Robert Browning
(1812–1889, English poet)

*I*n spite of the warm afternoon sunshine the solitary cottages, low lying on the brook, looked cold and damp, but the apples hung bright on the trees in the cottage gardens and a Virginia creeper burned like fire in crimson upon the wall, crimson among the green.

Francis Kilvert
(1840–1879, clergyman)

*H*e told of the magnolia spread
High as a cloud, high over head!
The cypress and her spire;
—Of flowers that with one scarlet gleam
Cover a hundred leagues, and seem
To set the hills on fire.

William Wordsworth
(1770–1850, English poet)

*B*efore all else, we city gardeners must learn to disregard the discouraging, then proceed to confound the cynical. Country cousins with quantities of land would have us believe that only very few or very boring plants can endure a city—or, worse, that no "good" plant deserves this fate. Yet it seems whenever I hear of a species that "won't survive" an urban site, that plant is the pride of the next city garden I visit—from arugula to water lilies, and beach plumb too.

Linda Yang,
b. 1937,
The City Gardener's Handbook

A hedge doesn't grow down—it follows the sun.

Gus Yearicks
(essayist)

*R*oses, ranged in valiant row,
I will never think that she passed you by!
She loves you noble roses, I know;
But, yonder, see, where the rock-plants lie!

Robert Browning
(1812–1889, English poet)

*M*en only doth smell and take delight in the odors of flowers and sweet things.

William Bullein
(English physician, medical writer)

What does he plant who plants a tree?
He plants the friend of sun and sky.
A nation's growth from sea to sea
Stirs in his heart who plants a tree.

Henry Cuyler Bunner
(1855–1896, American journalist, writer)

Though nothing can bring back the hour
Of splendor in the grass, or glory in
the flower.

William Wordsworth
(1770–1850, English poet)

"Things are crowding up out of the earth," she ran
on in a hurry. "And there are flowers uncurling and
buds on everything and the green veil has covered
nearly all the gray and the birds are in such a hurry
about their nests for fear they may be too late that
some of them are even fighting for places in the secret
garden . . .

Frances Hodgson Burnett,
1849–1924,
The Secret Garden

How does the meadow flower its
bloom unfold?
Because the lovely little flower is free
Down to its root, and, in that freedom, bold.

William Wordsworth
(1770–1850, English poet)

257

*I*n the Italian garden
tulips, iris wait
for the old bent gardener
to open the heavy gate.

Humbert Wolfe
(1886–1940, English poet)

*F*or oft, when on my couch I lie
In vacant or in pensive mood
They flash upon that inward eye
Which is the bliss of solitude;
And then my heart with pleasure fills
And dances with the daffodils.

William Wordsworth
(1770–1850, English poet)

*A*ll work is as seed sown; it grows and spreads; and
sows itself anew.

Thomas Carlyle
(1795–1881, British essayist, historian)

*W*ee, modest, crimson-tipped flower,
Thou's met me in an evil hour,
For I may crush among the stour
Thy slender stem:
To spare the now is past my pow'r,
Thou bonie gem.

Robert Burns
(1759–1796, Scottish poet)

*O*ur attitude toward plants is a singularly narrow one. If we see any immediate utility in a plant we foster it. If for any reason we find the presence undesirable or merely a matter of indifference, we may condemn it to destruction forthwith.

Rachel Carson,
The Silent Spring
(1907–1964, marine biologist, environmentalist)

*I*f you want to identify plants expertly, you should spend a lot of time surreptitiously reading labels.

Geoffrey B. Charlesworth,
The Opinionated Gardener

*I*t is the destiny of certain plants to make the world in which they live a pleasanter and more gracious place. Indeed it is such as these that often endow a garden with particular charm. Like mist in the distance they soften and enhance the landscape, bestow grace and a little sense of mystery . . . As I consider this type of plant there comes to mind corydalis, lovely in shadowed walls . . .

Louise Beebe Wilder,
What Happens in My Garden

*T*he plants you tend become the companions that need you, they mitigate the early evening hours, surely the loneliest time of day; they welcome your return after an absence.

Helen Van Pelt Wilson, b. 1901,
Helen Van Pelt Wilson's
Own Garden & Landscape Book

*F*lowers are happy things.

P. G. Wodehouse
(1881–1975, English writer, humorist)

*M*any things grow in the garden that were never sowed there.

Chinese proverb

*F*lowers are as common in the country as people are in London.

Oscar Wilde
(1854–1900, English poet, dramatist)

*T*he "one color" gardens that are at present enjoying a good deal of favor seem to me satisfactory mainly as achievements. The are apt to be monotonous in effect, and are seldom truly harmonious.

Louise Beebe Wilder,
Color in My Garden

*T*he cost of a plant depends on the number
of blossoms.
For a fine flower, a hundred pieces of damask;
For a cheap flower, five bits of silk.

Po Chu-I
(772–846 A.D., Chinese poet)

*F*lowers are lovely; love is flower-like;
Lovely flowers are the smiles of God's goodness.

Samuel Wilberforce
(1759–1833, English religious leader)

The roses lie upon the grass
Like little shreds of crimson silk.

Oscar Wilde
(1854–1900,
English poet, dramatist)

I took money and bought flowering trees
And planted them out on the bank to the
        east of the keep.
I simply bought whatever had most blooms,
Not caring whether peach, apricot, or plum
a hundred fruits all mixed up together;
A thousand branches, flowering in
        due rotation;

Po Chu-I
(ninth century Chinese poet)

For me the jasmine buds unfold
And silver daisies star the lea,
The crocus hoards the sunset gold,
And the wild rose breathes for me.

Florence Earle Coates
(1850–1927, poet)

Through the open door
A drowsy smell of flowers—gray heliotrope
And white sweet clover, and shy mignotte
Comes faintly in, and silent chorus leads
To the pervading symphony of peace.

John Greenleaf Whittier
(1807–1892, American poet)

261

*I*n the dooryard fronting an old farm-
     house near the white-wash'd palings,
Stands the lilac-bush tall-growing with
     heart-shaped leaves of rich green,
With many a pointed blossom rising delicate,
     with the perfume strong I love,
With every leaf a miracle.

Walt Whitman,
"When Lilacs in the Dooryard Last Bloomed"
(1819–1892, American poet)

*A*long the river's summer walk,
The withered tufts of asters nod;
And trembles on its arid stalk
The hoar plume of the golden-rod.
And on the ground a sombre fir,
And azure-studded juniper,
The silver birch its buds of purple shows,
And scarlet berries tell where bloomed
     the sweet wild rose!

John Greenleaf Whittier
(1807–1892, American poet)

*O*ur vegetable garden is coming along well, with
radishes and beans up, and we are less worried about
revolution than we used to be.

E. B. White
(1899–1985, American essayist)

*P*otatoes are very interesting folks. I think they must
see a lot of what is going on in the earth. They have so
many eyes.

Opal Whiteley
(American diarist)

*L*ong and often hazardous journeys to find them.

James Underwood Crockett,
Flowering Shrubs
(1915–1979, American horticulturist)

*G*od wrote his loveliest poem on the day he made the first tall silver poplar tree.

Grace Noll Crowell
(1877–1969, American poet)

*A*re these the old-time meadows? Yes the wild-grape scents the air; The breadth of ripened orchard. Still is incense everywhere.

Thomas Welsh
(writer)

*T*he masterpiece should appear as the flower to the painter—perfect in its bud as in its bloom—with no reason to explain its presence—no mission to fulfill—a joy to the artist, a delusion to the philanthropist—a puzzle to the botanist—an accident of sentiment and alliteration to the literary man.

James McNeill Whistler
(1834–1903, American painter)

*G*ardening has a magical quality when you are a child. You plant little dry brown bulbs in the fall, and while they are sleeping through the winter you almost forget about them. But in the spring they remember to come up as bright yellow and purple crocuses.

Barbara Damrosch,
Theme Gardens
(American landscape designer) 1982

*I*t has always pleased me to exalt plants in the scale of organized beings.

Charles Darwin
(1809–1882, English naturalist)

*O*h! No man knows through what wild centuries roves back the rose.

Walter De la Mare,
By Any Other Name—A Book of Roses
(1873–1956, English poet)

*O*ne could not die for you. To be sure, an ordinary passerby would think that my rose just looked just like you—the rose that belongs to me. But in herself alone she is more important than all the hundreds of you other roses; because it is she that I have watered; because it is she that I have put under the glass globe; because it is she that I have sheltered behind the screen; because it is for her that I have killed the cater-pillars; because it is she that I have listened to when she grumbled, or boasted, or even sometimes when she said nothing. Because she is my rose.

Antoine de Saint Exupéry,
The Little Prince
(French aviator, novelist)

*W*hen will the world know that peace and propaga-tion are the two most delightful things in it?

Horace Walpole
(1717–1797, English earl, writer)

$\mathcal{B}$ut where, you ask, where were the
vegetables?—
the dues each rustic from however clenched
soil should extort—potatoes duly trenched,
the buxom cabbage, onions well-trod,
and marrows rounding to the glory of God
at harvest festival—you name not these.

Sylvia Townsend Warner
(1893–1978, English novelist)

$\mathcal{T}$he man around the corner keeps experimenting
with new flowers every year, and now has quite an
extensive list of things he can't grow.

William Vaughn
(1577–1641, English poet, colonial pioneer)

$\mathcal{M}$an is related to plants as all living things are
related.

Josephine Von Miklos, 1900–1972, and Evelyn Fiore,
The History, the Beauty, the Riches
of the Gardener's World

$\mathcal{A}$ slight, pretty flower that grows on any ground,
and flowers pledge no allegiance to banners of any
man.

Alice Walker, b. 1944,
"The Child Who Favored Daughter,"
Love & Trouble: Stories of Black Women

$\mathcal{O}$ft in some dull dark corner blooms a flower.

Francois Coppeé
(1842–1908, French writer)

*F*lowers are words which even a babe may understand.

Bishop Arthur Cleveland Coxe
(religious leader, poet, writer)

*O*h, the green things growing, the green
    things growing,
The faint sweet smell of the green things
    growing!
I should like to live, whether I smile or grieve,
Just to watch the happy life of my green
    things growing.

Dinah Maria Mulock Craik
(1826–1887, English novelist)

*O*ft in a flower love's secret hidden lies.

Marceline Desbordes-Valmore
(French actress, poet)

*F*riendship is a sheltering tree.

Samuel Taylor Coleridge
(1772–1834, English poet, critic)

*W*e are closer to the vegetable kingdom than we know; it is not for us alone that mint, thyme, sage, and rosemary exhale "crush me and eat me!"–for us that opium poppy, coffee-berry, tea-plant and vine perfect themselves? Their aim is to be absorbed by man, although they can achieve it only by attaching themselves to roast mutton.

Cyril Connolly, The Unquiet Grave
(1903–1974, English essayist, critic, novelist)

$\mathcal{T}$he flowers taught me many lessons that I only fully understood much later. In experiencing growing my own flower garden and the whole process of planting the seeds, watching them grow, flower, fade and make seed, I learned about the cycles of life.

Denise Diamond, Living with Flowers

$\mathcal{C}$reeping on where time has been a rare old plant is the ivy green.

Charles Dickens, "The Ivy Green"
(1812–1870, English novelist)

$\mathcal{I}$t is as sprightly as the daffodil, as colorful as the rose, as resolute as the zinnia, as delicate as the chrysanthemum, as aggressive as the petunia, as ubiquitous as the violet, and as stately as the snap-dragon. It beguiles the senses and ennobles the spirit of man . . . Since it is native to America, and nowhere else in the world, and common to every state in the Union, I present the American marigold for designation as the national floral emblem of our country.

Everett M. Dirksen
(1896–1969, American political leader)

$\mathcal{L}$avender, sweet-briar, orris. Here
    shall Beauty make her pomander,
Are sweet-balls for to lay in clothes
That wrap her as the leaves the rose.

Katherine Tynan
(1861–1931, Irish poet, novelist)

$\mathscr{I}$ don't share the opinion of those people who think that people who love flowers are necessarily good. Even those who love animals are not always so; certain people love flowers and animals because they are incapable of getting along with their fellow human beings.

Sigrid Undset
(1882–1949, writer)

$\mathscr{C}$ut herbs just as the dew does dry,
Tie them loosely and hang them high
If you plan to store away,
Stir the leaves a bit each day.

Unknown
American Farmer, 1842

$\mathscr{A}$nd because the breath of flowers is far sweeter in the air than in the hand, therefore nothing is more fit for that delight than to know what be the flowers and plants that do best perfume the air.

Katherine Tynan
(1861–1931, Irish poet, novelist)

$\mathscr{T}$he botanists and the florists are distinct persons, and their theories are quite opposite one another. The botanist delights in nature—the florist in art.

Walter Elder (writer)

$\mathscr{W}$hatever a man's age, he can reduce it several years by putting a bright-colored flower in his buttonhole.

Mark Twain
(1835–1910, American writer)

*H*ow cunningly nature hides every wrinkle of her inconceivable antiquity under roses and violets and morning dew!

Ralph Waldo Emerson
(1803–1882, American philosopher, writer)

*P*lants are the young of the world, vessels of health and vigor; but they grope ever upward towards consciousness; the trees are imperfect men, and seem to bemoan their imprisonment, rooted in the ground.

Ralph Waldo Emerson
(1803–1882, American philosopher, writer)

*F*ruit gathered too timely will taste of the wood will shrink and be bitter, and seldom prove good.

Thomas Tusser
(1524–1580, English agricultural writer, poet)

*H*istory records the names of royal bastards, but cannot tell us the origin of wheat.

Jean Henri-Fabre
(1823–1915, French entomologist)

*T*he boughs of the oak are roaring inside the acorn shell.

Charles Tomlinson
b. 1927, (poet)

*A*ll the wars of the world, all the Caesars, have not the staying power of a lily in a cottage border . . . the immortality of marbles and of miseries is a vain, small thing compared to the immortality of a flower that blooms and is dead by dusk.

Reginald Farrer, 1880–1920,
The Rainbow Bridge

I'm trying to understand how an empty tube behind a flower swells to fruit, how leaves twisting from trees are pieces of last year's fire spoiling to humus.

Gretel Erlich,
The Solace of Open Spaces

To analyze the charms of flowers is like dissecting music; it is one of those things which it is far better to enjoy, than to attempt to understand.

Henry Theodore Tuckerman
(American critic, essayist, poet)

The careless eye can find no grace,
No beauty in the scaly folds,
Nor see within the dark embrace
What latent loveliness it holds.
Yet in that bulb, those sapless scales,
The lily wraps her silver vest.

Mary Tighe
(Irish poet)

Flowers perish so fast that often we should scarcely value their lovely fragility except as the symbol and token of something quite as lovely and not so frail.

Oscar W. Firkens
(writer)

One of the attractive things about flowers is their beautiful reserve.

Henry David Thoreau
(1817–1862, American naturalist, writer)

I sometimes think that never blows so red
The rose as where some buried Caesar bled;
That every Hyacinth the garden wears
Dropt in her lap from some once lovely head.

Edward Fitzgerald
(1809–1883, English poet, translator)

271

*N*othing grows in our garden, only washing and babies.

Dylan Thomas
(b. 1913, Welsh writer)

... *T*he public must learn how to cherish the nobler and rarer plants, and to plant the aloe, able to wait a hundred years for its bloom, or its garden will contain, presently, nothing but potatoes and pot-herbs.

Margaret Fuller
(1810–1850, American poet, writer)

(Standing in a field of uncountable wildflowers, he asked:)

*M*y good man, have you never looked into the heart of a flower?

Clark Gable
(1901–1960, American actor)

A large pearly shell of the whelk tribe was given me a few years ago. I did not know what to do with it ... In itself it was beautiful, a mass of glimmering rainbows. I bored three holes in its edge and suspended it from one of the severely simple chandeliers with almost invisible wires. I keep it filled with water and in it arrange sometimes clusters of monthly honeysuckle sparingly; the hues of the flowers and the shell mingle and blend divinely.

Celia Thaxter,
An Island Garden

*N*ear my own seat in a sofa corner at one of the south windows stands yet another small table . . . On this are gathered every day all the rarest and loveliest flowers as they blossom, that I may touch them, dwell on them, breathe their delightful fragrance and adore them.

Celia Thaxter,
An Island Garden

*W*orld unto world unto world remolded.
This is the seed, compact of God,
Wherein all mystery is enfolded.

Georgie Starbuck Galbraith,
"On a Seed" (writer)

*T*his was the goal of the leaf and the root.
For this did the blossom burn its hour.
This little grain is the ultimate fruit.
This is the awesome vessel of power.

Wearing all that wright
Of learning lightly like a flower.

Alfred, Lord Tennyson
(1809–1892, English poet)

*T*he ancient Greeks crowned themselves with rosemary wreaths during exams, believing the herb would improve their memory.

Barbara Gallup and Deborah Reich,
The Complete Book of Totally Topiary, *1988*
(horticulturists, writers)

*F*lower in the crannied wall,
I pluck you out of the crannies,
I hold you here, root and all, in my hand,
Little flower—but I could understand
What you are, root and all, and all in all,
I should know what God and Man is.

Alfred, Lord Tennyson
(1809–1892, English poet)

*E*arth receives the seed and guards it,
Trustfully it dies:
Then what teeming life rewards it,
For self sacrifice.
With green leaf and clustering blossom
Clad, or golden fruit,
See it from the earth's cheerless bosom
Ever sunward shoot.

Diwan-I-Shams-I-Tabriz
(poet)

*A*nd God said, let the earth bring forth grass, the
herb yielding seed, and the fruit tree yielding fruit
after his kind, whose seed is in itself, upon the earth:
and it was so.

Genesis 1:11

*Y*ou should go to a pear-tree for pears, not to an elm.

Publilius Syrus
(Latin writer)

*Y*ou may as well expect pears from an elm.

Geruanteu (writer)

*V*egetable seed catalogs have replaced the penny candy store. The fireballs, the root-beer barrels, and the licorice whips aren't sold at the corner anymore. Now the sweets are sold by seed companies instead. There's "candystick" and "sweet slice" and "sugar rock," but these aren't types of candy, they are varieties of sweet corn, cucumber and musk melon.

> Roger B. Swain,
> Earthly Pleasures
> *(biologist, TV host)*

*V*iolet, violet, sparkling with dew,
Down in the meadow land wild, where you grew,
How did you come by the beautiful blue,
With which your soft petals unfold?

> *Hannah F. Gould,*
> *from* The Old Farmers Almanac
> *(American poet)*

*H*e wanted a flower garden of yellow daisies because they were the only flower which resembled the face of his wife and the sun of his love.

> *Bessie Head, 1937–1986,*
> Maru

*W*hat, has the cypress perished? by Narvan's
flowers the eye still bless,
The tulips gaudy gloom is o'er, but then mark
the jasmine's loudness.

> *Anwar-I-Suheili*
> *(poet)*

From a plant's point of view extra seed is just insurance that some will germinate, but to a gardener the sight of two- or three-year-old packets still partially filled with now-defunct seed is depressing. Dreams that died on the shelf.

Roger B. Swain,
The Practical Gardener
(biologist, TV host)

Fair daffodils, we weep to see
You haste away so soon.

Robert Herrick
(1591–1674, English poet)

The amen! of nature is always a flower.

Oliver Wendell Holmes, Sr.
(1841–1935, writer)

A rose is a rose is a rose.

Gertrude Stein
(1874–1946, American poet, novelist)

When you brought the roses, I felt something
Stir in me that I thought was dead
Forever.

From "The Subject Was Roses"
Frank D. Gilroy
(writer)

Thus by the rose the garden's crown is worn
Because, though soft, it couches on a Thorn.

Anwar-I-Suheili (poet)

Fair, an, fair, is the Sunny Orange Garden,
Secret and shady, scented and green,
Gold, red gold, are the oranges in clusters,
Fragrant and bright in their ripened sheen.

Laurence Hope
(1864–1904, English poet)

Oh, tell me how my garden grows,
Where I no may take delight,
And if some dream of me it knows,
Who dream of it by day and night.

Mildred Howells
(painter, poet)

Another gay garland
For my faire love of lilies and of roses
Bound tru-love-wise with a blue silk ribband
And let them make great store of bridal posies.

Edmund Spenser
(1552–1599, English poet)

To throw flowers is to offer a promise
The lightest signs—the greatest sufferings
My woes, my happiness, my little sacrifices
There are my flowers!

Saint Therest
(the "Little Flower")

277

*S*ixteen summers had she seen,
A rose-bud just unsealing.

Mary Howitt (English poet)

*W*e're serious but not solemn about potatoes here.
The potato has lots of eyes, but no mouth. That's
where I come in.

E. Thomas Hughes,
founder, Potato Museum, Washington, D. C.

*A*nyone can cultivate an herbaceous border, but to
grow a natural garden is an art and a science.

F. S. Smythe, 1900–1949,
The Valley of Flowers

*I*t often comes as a surprise to sophisticated citizens
of developed countries to realize how much they
depend on plants.

Anthony Huxley,
Green Inheritance (botanist, writer)

*N*ot useless are ye flowers; though made
      for pleasure,
Blooming o'er fields, and wave by day
      and night
From every source your sanction bids
      me treasure
Harmless delight.

Horace Smith
(1808–1893, English poet, parodist)

*I*f there were nothing else to trouble us, the fate of flowers would make us sad.

John Lancaster Spalding
(1609–1670, writer)

*J*ust simply alive,
　　　Both of us, I
　　　And the poppy.

Haiku by Issa
(Oriental poet)

*W*e have loved plants, and sometimes worshipped them, all through history. Far more than animals, plants have been symbols of the earth's life force and have provided solace to the human race.

Anthony Huxley,
Green Inheritance
(botanist, writer)

*T*hen, jealous Nature, yield the palm to me,
To me thy pride its early triumph owes;
Though *thy* rude workmanship produced
　　　the tree,
'T was *education* formed the perfect rose.

Charlotte Smith
(English poet, novelist)

*T*he greatest service which can be rendered any country is to add a useful plant to its culture.

Thomas Jefferson
(1743–1826, American president)

$\mathscr{I}$ love the topiary art, with its trimness and primness, and its open or oval of its artificial character. It repudiates at the first glance the skulking and cowardly "celare artum" principle, and, in its vegetable sculpture, is the properest transition from the architecture of the house to the natural beauties of the grove and paddock.

T. James,
Carthusian

$\mathscr{T}$he rose bushes were planted along the sides of the road which ran through our village and were greatly admired by the passersby, but it was strongly impressed on us that a rose was useful, not ornamental. It was not intended to please us by its color or its odor. Its mission was to be made into rosewater, and if we thought of it in any other way we were making an idol of it and thereby imperilling our souls.

A sister in a Shaker community
(American)

$\mathscr{T}$his bud of love, by summer's ripening breath,
May prove a beauteous flower when next we meet.

William Shakespeare
(1564–1616, English dramatist, poet)

$\mathscr{W}$ho has told you that the fruit belies the flower?
For the fruit you have not tasted, and the flower
you know but by report.

Murasaki Shikibu
(Oriental poet)

Out of this nettle, danger, we pluck this flower, safety.

William Shakespeare
(1564–1616, English dramatist, poet)

[Ivy is] a precious and beautiful climbing plant . . . [whose] nobility of form and foliage is a desirable accompaniment to good architecture.

Gertrude Jekyll and Lawrence Weaver,
Gardens for Small Country Houses, *1981*

Your flowers, trees, and shrubs are now planted— the vegetables too . . . you gaze at the perfection of your handiwork and *think* something like, okay, I've done *my* bit, so now it's *your* turn—grow! With one more loving glance, you turn away, ready for a hot shower and a cold martini.

Pamela Jones,
How Does Your Garden Grow?
(professional gardener, landscape artist)

"A grape-fruit in the morning will keep your brows from horning," they sing in New York, which is perhaps a little nearer Eden than is London.

Ford Maddox Ford
From Provence
(1873–1939, English writer)

*F*ruit unripe, sticks on the tree;
But fall, unshaken, when they mellow be.

William Shakespeare
(1564–1616, English dramatist, poet)

*M*r. John Bartram is an Englishman, who lives in the country about four miles from Philadelphia . . . He has in several successive years made frequent excursions into different distant parts of North America, with an intention of gathering all sorts of plants which are scarce and little known. Those which he found he has planted in his own botanical garden and likewise sent over their seeds or fresh roots to England. We owe to him the knowledge of many rare plants which he first found and which were never known before. He has shown great judgement and an attention which lets nothing escape unnoticed. Yet with all these qualities he is to be blamed for his negligence, for he did not care to write down his numerous and useful observations.

Peter Kalm
(friend of John Bartram, English botanist)

*T*he love of flowers is really the best teacher of how to grow and understand them.

Max Schiling
(writer)

*T*o gild refined gold, to paint the lily, to throw perfume on the violet . . . is wasteful and ridiculous.

William Shakespeare
(1564–1616, English dramatist, poet)

I cannot see what flowers are at my feet,
Nor what soft incense hangs upon the boughs,
But in embalmed darkness, guess each sweet.

John Keats
(1795–1821, English poet)

A heaven-sent gift and blessing is the rose
Its grace inspireth aspirations high
Oh flower girl, why the rose for silver sell?
Or what more precious with its price can buy?

Kisa'i (Oriental poet)

*I*f I had but two loaves of bread, I would sell one
and buy hyacinths, for they would feed my soul.

The Koran

*W*hen you look at a flower, at a color, without naming it, with like or dislike, without any screen between you and the thing you see as a flower, without the word, without thought, then the flower has an extraordinary color and beauty. But when you look at a flower through botanical knowledge, when you say: "This is a rose," you have already conditioned your response.

Jiddu Krishnamurti
(1895–1986, Indian Hindu philosopher)

$\mathcal{T}$he fact remains, nevertheless, that the herbalist did employ a considerable number of plants whose physiological effects were genuine, are still recognized and, in come cases, are still commonly prescribed.

Joseph Wood Krutch, Herbal
(1893–1970, American naturalist)

$\mathcal{S}$ome flowers spoke with strong and powerful violets, which proclaimed in accents trumped-tongued, "I am beautiful, and I rule," others murmured, in tones scarcely audible, but exquisitely soft and sweet, "I am little, and I am beloved."

George Sand,
Consuelo
(1804–1876, French novelist)

$\mathcal{T}$hus botany . . . is primarily the art of discovering the special virtue of each plant for the cure of one or another of the ills with which mankind is threatened.

Joseph Wood Krutch,
Herbal
(1893–1970, American naturalist)

$\mathcal{I}$ now have, amid hostas and fernery, fifty new plants, in a variety of kinds. Some, like royal ferns, ostrich ferns and cinnamon ferns, are huge and so prehistoric-looking that I would not be surprised to lift a frond and discover a baby dinosaur sitting in its protection.

Allen Lacy
(American garden writer)

*H*ow fair the flowers unaware
That do not know what beauty is!
Fair, without knowing they are fair;
With poets and gazelles they share
Another world than this.

Vita Sackville-West
(1892–1962, British poet, novelist)

*T*he rose spoke of burning loves, the lily of her chaste delight; the superb magnolia told of pure enjoyment and lofty pride; and the lovely little hepatica related the pleasure of a simple and returned existence.

George Sand, Consuelo
(1804–1876, French novelist)

This little space which scented box encloses
Is blue with lupins and is sharp with thyme.

Vita Sackville-West
(1892–1962, British poet, novelist)

Plants came to be grown not just for food but for their beauty and for their medicinal or magical properties. The choice of plants and organization of a garden often expressed this duality of purpose.

Librairie Larousse, Gardening & Gardens

Flowers seem intended for the solace of ordinary humanity.

John Ruskin
(1819–1900, English critic, artist, social reformer)

Water in a garden adds movement, light and sound; it also makes it possible to grow plants which are otherwise utterly out of the question.

Reader's Digest Guide to Creative Gardening

O'er folded blooms,
On swirls of musk,
The beetle booms adorn the glooms
And bumps along the dusk.

James Whitcomb Riley
(1849–1916, American poet)

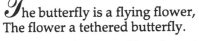

The butterfly is a flying flower,
The flower a tethered butterfly.

Ecouchard Le Brun (French poet)

It is a greater act of faith to plant a bulb than to plant a tree . . . It needs a great imagination to see in these weeded, colourless shapes the subtle curves of the iris reticulate or the tight locks of the hyacinth. At the time of bulb planting one most nearly approaches the state of mind of the mystic.

Clare Leighton (writer)

It is so wrong to think of the beauty of flowers only when they are at their height of blooming; bud and half developed flower, fading blossom and seed pod are lovely, and often more interesting.

Clare Leighton (writer)

Till you grow your own potatoes, you do not really begin to live. A house without a garden is a temporary home.

Richard Le Gallienne
(1866–1947, English poet, critic)

In a very real sense, plants are the only sustainable resource we have: cherishing it, preserving it, and learning to use this resource more efficiently are necessary ingredients for human prosperity in the future.

Peter H. Raven, Foreward,
Wily Violets & Underground Orchids,
by Peter Bernhardt
(director of Missouri Botanical Garden)

*W*hen you walk up to a flower and really look at it, with the idea of a propagation in mind, you realize how little you know.

Anne Raver
(garden columnist)

*F*lowers have a language all their own that transcends international barriers. As with music, there is also a timelessness about flowers and a sense of communication. They bring people together in the most enchanting ways, and isn't this what life is all about?

Princess Grace of Monaco, 1929–1982,
My Book of Flowers
(Grace Kelly)

*P*lants take away some of the anxiety and tension of the immediate NOW by showing us that there are enduring patterns in life.

Charles Lewis,
speech to the American Horticultural Society, 1985
(horticulturist)

*T*hrough primrose tofts, in that green bower,
The periwinkle trailed its wreaths;
And 'tis my faith that every flower
Enjoys the air it breathes.

Ernest Powson (writer)

. . . *S*hrubs overgrow paths. Sometimes you can move the path but if not, then girth control must be imposed.

Christopher Lloyd, b. 1938,
The Well Chosen Garden

The more time one devotes to growing plants, the more plants invade the home.

H. Peter Loewer,
Bringing the Outdoors In
(botanical author, artist)

For me huge flower masses hold no particular delight. Such effects could be created as easily by a house painter. An individual blossom, with its delicacies and magical personal distinction, affords me the greater pleasure.

Eden Phillpotts
(1862–1960, English novelist)

... A writer who gardens is sooner or later going to write a book about the subject—I take that as inevitable.

Eleanor Perenyi, b. 1918,
Green Thoughts: A Writer in the Garden

Sooner or later, after becoming involved with growing plants, the collecting urge appears from left field and we begin to wish for more.

H. Peter Loewer,
Bringing the Outdoors In
(botanical author, artist)

Like people, plants respond to extra attention.

H. Peter Loewer,
Bringing the Outdoors In
(botanical author, artist)

If you've never started seeds don't worry too much about it. Remember, nature has designed them to *want* to grow. You and the garden seeds have exactly the same goal—what could be more reassuring?

Ruth Page,
Ruth Page's Gardening Journal *(radio show host)*

Now draw the plan of our garden beds,
And outline the borders and the paths correctly.
We will scatter little words upon the paper,
Like seeds about to be planted.

Amy Lowell
(1874–1925, American poet, essayist, biographer)

[N]obody sees a flower—really—it is so small—we haven't time—and to see takes time like to have a friend takes time.

Georgia O'Keefe
(1887–1986, American painter)

Nature was surely in a gentle mood when she created the ferns.

Henry and Rebecca Northern,
Ingenious Kingdom

Flowers first broke up the prism and made the most subtle portion of our sight.

Maurice Maeterlinck
(1862–1949, Belgian poet, count, dramatist, essayist)

$\mathcal{P}$eople from a planet without flowers would think we must be mad with Joy the whole time to have such things about us.

Iris Murdoch
(b. 1919, British novelist)

$\mathcal{A}$nd the fruits will outdo what the flowers have promised.

François de Malherbe
(1553–1628, writer)

$\mathcal{I}$ will make you a bed of roses, and a thousand fragrant posies.

Kit Marlowe
(1564–1593, writer, poet)

$\mathcal{F}$lowers nodding gaily, scent in air,
Flowers poised, Flowers for the hair,
Sleepy Flowers, Flowers bold to stare—
O pick me some!

T. Sturge Moore
(1870–1944, British poet, illustrator)

$\mathcal{B}$lue thou art, intensely blue!
Flower! whence came thy dazzling hue?
When I opened first mine eye,
Upward glancing to the sky,
Straight way from the firmament
Was the sapphire brilliance sent.

James Montgomery
(1771–1854, English poet)

*S*ee how the flowers, as at parade,
Under their colours stand displayed:
Each regiment in order grows,
That of the Tulip, pink and rose.

Andrew Marvell
(1621–1678, English poet, satirist)

*P*erennials can be moved!! Many of them have trav-
eled long distances in our own garden. Had they
belonged to an airline travel club, I am sure a few
would have won a trip to Hawaii by now.

Frederick McGourty, Jr.,
American Horticulturist Magazine,
February 1985
(garden writer)

*T*he thicket's resistance to trespass, while everywhere formidable, stiffened considerably as it evolved
upward. Thick were intertwining mixtures of manzanita, California lilac, scrub oak, chamise.

John McPhee,
The Control of Nature
(American novelist)

*M*any fine flowers are cursed with atrocious
names. I'd just as soon call an iris "cystitis" as to call it
a name inspired by some gasbag politician or some
movie queen who wouldn't know her namesake's pis-
til from its stamens.

Julian R. Meade,
Bouquets & Bitters

*M*ore than anything I must have flowers, always,
always.

Claude Monet
(1840–1926, French painter)

*B*ut the fruit that will fall without shaking;
Indeed is too mellow for me.

Lady Mary Wortley Montagu
(1689–1762, English letter writer, poet)

*M*arigolds are bright and beautiful if, like cousins,
you don't have too many of them at once.

Henry Mitchell,
The Essential Earthman

I will be the gladdest thing under the sun!
I will touch a hundred flowers and not pick one.

Edna St. Vincent Millay
(American poet)

*H*ide me from the day's garish eye
While the bee with honied thigh,
That at her flowery work doth sing,
And the waters murmuring
With such consort as they keep.
Entice the dewy-feathered sleep.

John Milton
(1608–1674, English epic poet)

Author Index

Abbot, Charles C., 107
Acres, Slim, 247
Adams, Abigail, 47, 99
Adams, William Howard, 3, 4, 5
Addison, Joseph, 99
Aiken, Conrad, 47
Albee, John, 61
Alcott, Amos Bronson, 191
Alcott, Louisa May, 129
Aldrich, Thomas Bailey, 173
Allen's Almanack, 144
Allingham, William, 247
Altenberg, Peter, 171
Amiel, Henri Frederic, 1, 192
Anonymous, 1, 2, 48, 171, 172, 173, 193, 248
Anonymous (from "A Man of Words and Not of Deeds"), 48
Anonymous (from "Corners of Old Grey Gardens"), 129
Anonymous (Egypt), 192
Anonymous (from an Egyptian poem), 49
Anonymous (fifteenth-century German), 100
Anonymous (Nigeria), 192
Anonymous (Senegal/Gambia), 248
Anouilh, Jean, 193
Arab proverb, 194
Arnold, Matthew, 2, 100
Arnold, Oren, 130
Arnold, Sir Edwin, 129, 194
Arnow, Harriette, 131
Asemius, 2
Asmenius, 50
Attār, Farīd od-Dīn, 249
Attenborough, David, 249
Ausonius, Decimus Magnus, 131

Austein, Ralph, 3
Austin, Alfred, 2, 194

Bacall, Lauren, 51
Bacon, Francis, Sir, 195, 249
Bailey, Lee, 4, 195
Bailey, Liberty Hyde, 4, 52, 250
Balfour, Clara L., 23
Ball, Jeff, 53, 100, 101
Baltimore Sun, 51
Barr, Charles, 52
Barrette, Roy, 101, 102
Barrie, James Matthew, 131
Barrington, Shute, Bishop, 173
Bartram, John, 52
Bartram, William, 109
Bashō, 5
Beach, Joseph W., 196
Beard, James, 51, 53
Beaton, Cecil, 52
Beecher, Henry Ward, 5, 196, 197, 250, 251
Bell, Henry Glassford, 197
Bellaman, Henry, 5, 198
Belleau, Remy, 132
Benjamin, Park, 198
Bennett, Dan, 251
Bennett, Ida D., 53
Benson, A. C., 103
Bernhardt, Peter, 54, 199
Bernstein, Al, 132
Berry, Wendell, 50, 54, 82
Beston, Henry, 199
Better Homes & Gardens New Garden Book, 103
Billings, Josh, 199
Bird, Christopher, 117, 200

Bishop, Jim, 130
Black, Doris, 150
Blake, Peter, 201
Blake, William, 55, 104, 173, 202, 203
Blanchan, Neltje, 134
Blessington, Marguerite, 173, 252
Blount, Thomas Pope, Sir, 202
Boese, Paul, 55
Bombeck, Erma, 57, 58
Borland, Hal, 24, 55, 56, 57, 105, 133, 134, 176, 177, 252
Boulton, Sir Harold Edwin, 202
Bower, Kenneth, 204
Bradstreet, Anne, 135
Bramah, Ernest, 205
Breck, Joseph, 57, 205, 254
Bridges, Robert, 136, 205, 251
Brody, Jane, 50
Brontë, Charlotte, 252
Brooke, Frances, 255
Brooke, Rupert, 249, 250
Brookes, John, 7, 49, 56, 59, 206, 207, 208
Brooks, Gwendolyn, 137
Broomfield, Louis, 60
Brown, Alice, 9, 207
Brown, Thomas Edward, 6, 208
Browne, Thomas, Sir, 1, 7, 208
Browning, Elizabeth Barrett, 176
Browning, Robert, 8, 137, 177, 255, 256
Bryant, William Cullen, 7, 105, 138, 139, 140, 178, 209
Buczacki, Stefan, 61, 140, 141
Bullein, William, 256
Bunner, Henry Cuyler, 257
Burke, Edmund, 106
Burnett, Frances Hodgson, 8, 179, 257
Burns, Robert, 178, 179, 258
Burroughs, John, 54, 132, 141
Burton, Richard Francis, Sir, 9, 281
Butler, William, Dr., 247
Buxton, Thomas F., Sir, 4

Campbell, Jane Montgomery, 171
Campion, Thomas, 9
Čapek, Karel, 10, 107

Capote, Truman, 10
Carlyle, Thomas, 258
Carman, William Bliss, 11, 174, 210
Carson, Rachel, 259
Carter, Jimmy, 210
Cather, Willa, 211
Caudell, Harry M., 61
Chadwick, Janet, 53, 99
Chagall, Marc, 211
Charles, Prince, (H.R.H. Prince of Wales), 93
Charlesworth, Geoffrey B., 259
Chaucer, Geoffrey, 11, 142, 180, 212
Chesterton, G. K., 212
Child, Julia, 62
Child, Lydia Maria, 213
Chinese proverb, 1, 12, 92, 142, 260
Chora, 108
Church, Thomas D., 12, 13
Cicero, 214
Clare, John, 14, 106, 107, 138
Clark, June, 2
Clopinel, J., 14
Coates, Florence Earle, 261
Cobbett, William, 55, 56, 214, 216
Cole, Samuel Valentine, 216
Cole, Thomas, 217
Coleridge, Samuel Taylor, 143, 266
Colette, 62, 63
Columbus, Christopher, 217
Confucius, 62
Connolly, Cyril, 143, 217, 266
Cook, Clarence Chatham, 142
Coppée, Francois, 265
Corot, Jean-Baptiste-Camille, 217
Coughlin, Robert M., 110
Cowley, Abraham, 15, 181, 218
Cowper, William, 5, 219
Coxe, Arthur Cleveland, Bishop, 266
Craik, Dinah Maria Mulock, 219, 266
Crashau, Richard, 144
Creasy, Rosalind, 108, 124, 220
Crocket, Jim, 16
Crockett, James Underwood, 263
Croft-Cooke, Rupert, 181

Crowe, Sylvia, 16
Crowell, Grace Noll, 263
Cruso, Thalassa, 17
Cuppy, Will, 111

Dairs, William T., 219
D'Alverne, Pierre, 144
Damrosch, Barbara, 17, 64, 65, 220, 263
Daniel Arnaut, 145
Dante, 17
Dario, Ruben, 145
Darwin, Charles, 264
D'Aurenga, Raimbaut, 182
Davenport, Guy, 221
Davidson, A. K., 12
Davies, Robertson, 65
Davies, W. H., 66
De Berceo, 66
De Herrera, Fernando, 182
dc la Barca, Pedro Calderon, 180
de la Cruz, Juana Ines, 238
De la Mare, Walter, 18, 264
de la Renta, Oscar, 248
De Laprade, Victor, 145
De Lisle, Leconte, 145
de Malherbe, François, 291
De Nerval, Gerard, 67, 111
De Regnier, Henri, 29
De Salery, Francis, Saint, 72
De Ventadour, Bernard, 146
Desbordes-Valmore, Marceline, 221, 266
D'Este, Beatrice, 66
Diamond, Denise, 18, 267
Dickens, Charles, 267
Diettrich, Fritz, 148, 184
Dirksen, Everett M., 267
Disraeli, Benjamin, 67
Dobson, Henry Austin, 149
Dodsley, Robert, 150
D'Orleans, Charles, 135
Douglas, James, 19
Downing, Andrew Jackson, 19
Drinkwater, John, 151
Driscoll, Louise, 20, 152, 184, 222
Drury, Ian, 68

Dunce, Oliver Bell, 184
Durrell, Gerald, 222

Earle, Alice Morse, 20
Ecclesiastes, verses from, 153, 185
Edward VI, King, 23
Edwards, Jonathan, 21
Elder, Walter, 268
Eliot, George, 68
Ely, Helena Rutherford, 223, 224
Emerson, Ralph Waldo, 22, 69, 112, 153, 154,
  225, 226, 227, 269
Erasmus, Desiderius, 21
Erlich, Gretel, 270
Ernst, Ruth Shaw, 70, 154, 185, 186
Erskine, John, 22
Evans, Howard Ensign, 130
Evans, Howard Signal, 108
Evans, Mary Page, 226
Evans, Minnie, 227
Evelyn, John, 23

Fabre, Jean-Henri, 269
Fane, Violet, 9, 24
Farmer's Almanac, 143, 176
  1846, 251
  1854, 252
  1872, 253
  1881, 60
  1887, 253
Farmer's Journal, Belfast, 71
Farrer, Reginald, 71, 125, 270
Feltwell, John, 124
Finch, Robert, 111, 155, 157
Fiore, Evelyn, 16, 115, 265
Firkens, Oscar W., 271
Fitzgerald, Edward, 228, 271
Fitzgerald, F. Scott, 155
Floyd, Keith, 49
Ford, Ford Maddox, 281
Forster, E. M., 156, 186
Fox, Helen Morgenthau, 71
Freeman, Orville L., 228
French proverb, 222
Freud, Sigmund, 25

Friend, Henry, 157
Frost, Robert, 112
Fukuonoka, Masanobu, 25
Fuller, Margaret, 272
Fuller, Thomas, 26, 72, 187, 201
Fyleman, Rose, 26

Gable, Clark, 272
Gabriel, Honoré, 229
Galbraith, Georgie Starbuck, 273
Gallup, Barbara, 26, 229, 230, 273
Galsworthy, Frank, 27
Gandhi, Rajiv, 230
Gannett, Lewis, 157
Garnet, Frances, 73
Garrison, Theodosia, 230
Gascoigne, George, 231
Genesis, verses from, 27, 201, 274
George, Jean, 113
Gerard, John, 28
Geruanteu, 274
Gibbons, Euell, 157
Gide, André, 73
Gilroy, Frank D., 276
Giltinan, Caroline, 158
Gissing, George, 188
Goode, Jeanne, 159
Gorman, Judy, 74
Gould, Hannah F., 275
Gover, Richard, 74
Grace, H.R.H. Princess of Monaco, 32, 93,
    288
Grange, John, 75
Gray, Thomas, 159
Grayson, Daniel, 130
Grigson, Geoffrey, 62
Grimaed, Nicholas, 28
Guest, C. Z., 29, 161
Gundacker, Robert, 29
Gurney, Dorothy, 30
Gutterman, Arthur, 75

Hāfez, 76
Hagan, Patti, 113
Halpi, Arthur, Sir, 31

Hamilton, Geoff, 77
Hammer, Philene, 160
Hartsock, Ernest, 231
Hathaway, Katharine Butler, 161
Hawthorne, Nathaniel, 188
Hayes, Helen, 130
Hazlitt, W., 232
Head, Bessie, 275
Heidegger, Martin, 232
Henderson, Peter, 77
Hepburn, Katharine, 77, 233
Herbert, George, 10, 78, 233, 234
Herrick, Robert, 160, 162, 234, 276
Hewlett, Maurice, 31
Higginson, Thomas Wentworth, 113
Hillis, Burton, 78, 234
Holderlin, Friedrich, 162, 163
Holmes, Oliver Wendell, Sr., 163, 276
Homer, 189
Hope, Laurence, 277
Hopkins, Gerard Manley, 172, 235
Horace, 164, 235
Howard, Albert, Sir, 236
Howe, J. W., 164
Howells, Mildred, 62, 79, 277
Howitt, Mary, 32, 165, 278
Hubbard, Frank McKinney, 79, 80
Hubbard, Harlan, 109
Hudson, William Henry, 55, 108
Hughes, E. Thomas, 278
Hunt, Peter, 237
Hunt, William Lanier, 164
Husband, Francis Young, Sir, 77
Huxley, Anthony, 32, 33, 80, 114, 237, 278,
    279

Issa, 239, 279

James, I, King, 33
James, Henry, 137
James, T., 280
Jayasi, Malik Muhammad, 188
Jeffers, Robinson, 34
Jefferson, Thomas, 34, 80, 81, 238, 239, 240,
    279

Jeffries, Richard, 61, 109, 110, 166
Jekyll, Gertrude, 35, 36, 37, 241, 281
Jerrold, Douglas, 81
Jewett, Sarah Orne, 37
Johns, W. E., 37
Johnson, Lionel, 188
Johnson, Osa, 38
Johnson, Robert Underwood, 1
Johnson, Rossiter, 241
Johnson, Samuel, 242
Jones, Louise Seymour, 167
Jones, Pamela, 49, 114, 281
Jordan, William H., Jr., 114
Joubert, Joseph, 242
Joyes, Claire, 242
Judge, Jack, 115

Kalm, Peter, 39, 282
Kasmuneh, 82
Keats, John, 131, 135, 168, 169, 243, 283
Keller, Helen, 244
Kennedy, John F., 243
Kikaku, 244
Kilvert, Francis, 133, 138, 172, 244, 255
King, Louisa Yeomans, 40
King, Mrs. Francis, 168, 245
Kipling, Rudyard, 83, 169, 245, 250
Kisa'i, 283
Knapp, John Leonard, 64, 253, 254
Knickerbocker, Cholly, 84
Koran, The, 283
Krishnamurti, Jiddu, 283
Krutch, Joseph Wood, 241, 242, 284

Labe, Louise, 116, 240
Lacy, Allen, 40, 84, 85, 86, 240, 284
Ladew, Harvey, 48
Lamb, Charles, 41, 244
Langley, Batty, 41
Lappe, Frances Moore, 87
Larcom, Lucy, 243, 244
Latta, John E., Reverend, 241
Lawrence, D. H., 87
Lawrence, Elizabeth, 87, 88
Lawson, William, 88

Le Brun, Ecouchard, 287
Le Gallienne, Richard, 44, 117, 287
Lean, David, 89
Lees, Carlton B., 43, 44, 239, 240
Leighton, Clare, 45, 287
LeNôtre, André, 191
Leonard, John Knapp, 133
Leopold, Aldo, 239
Lessing, Doris, 90
Letts, Winifred, 169
Lewis, Charles, 288
Libraire Larousse, 42, 243, 286
Lincoln, Abraham, 238
Linnaeus, Carl, 91, 238
Lloyd, Christopher, 288
Loewer, H. Peter, 44, 45, 90, 91, 168, 169, 187, 289
Loleridge, Sarah, 168
Longfellow, Henry Wadsworth, 236
Lorang, Glen, 167
Lorns, W., 14
Lovejoy, Ann, 118
Lowell, Amy, 45, 167, 290
Lowell, James Russell, 91, 236, 237
Lucretius, 92
Lucus, E. V., 166
Lynd, Robert, 118, 119

MacArthur, Douglas, 92
McGiffert, Gertrude Huntington, 165
McGinley, Phyllis, 95, 232
McGourty, Frederick, Jr., 163, 164, 165, 292
MacLeish, Arch, 93
McMahon, Bernard, 162
McPhee, John, 292
Maeterlinck, Maurice, 43, 235, 290
Malloch, Douglas, 43
Mangan, James Clarence, 188
Mann, Thomas, 236
Manners, Miss, 94
Mansfield, Katherine, 94, 119, 235
Mao Tse-tung, 201
Marcus Aurelius, 101
Marlowe, Kit, 249, 291
Marranca, Bonnie, 42

Marsh, Anne, 41
Martial, 165
Martin, George A., 42
Marvell, Andrew, 3, 41, 94, 119, 233, 234, 292
Marx, Roberto Burle, 44
Meade, Julian R., 95, 292
Medici, Lorenzo de', 146
Mencken, H. L., 232
Mikes, George, 39
Millay, Edna St. Vincent, 78, 161, 162, 293
Miller, Lynden B., 40, 96
Milne, A. A., 95
Milton, John, 39, 121, 231, 293
Mitchell, Henry, 160, 161, 186, 293
Mitchell, Samuel, Dr., 38
Monet, Claude, 38, 293
Montagu, Mary Wortley, Lady, 293
Montaigne, Michel Eyquem de, 54, 70
Montgomery, James, 291
Moore, F. Frankfort, 37
Moore, T. Sturge, 291
Moore, Thomas, 38
Morley, Christopher, 120, 160
Morris, William, 35, 36
Morton, Sterling, 230
Muir, John, 121, 125, 200, 229
Mumford, Lewis, 229
Murdoch, Iris, 291

Nash, Ogden, 35, 96, 228
Native American saying, 216
Nelson, Victor, 97
New York Times editorial, 137
Newman, John Henry, Cardinal, 228
Nichols, Beverly, 227
Niebuhr, Reinhold, 97
Northern, Henry and Rebecca, 290
Notari, Louis, 227

O'Brien, Robert, 159
O'Keefe, Georgia, 290
Onitsura, 227
Ordish, George, 35
Osler, Mirabel, 223
Ostenso, Martha, 97

Page, Russell, 34, 123
Page, Ruth, 95, 96, 122, 124, 290
Palmer, Paul, 226
Parker, Dorothy, 159
Parker, Eric, 124
Parkinson, C. Northcote, 97
Pasternak, Boris, 226
Peattie, Donald Culross, 94, 125, 126, 132, 151, 224
Pepper, Jane G., 34
Perelman, S. J., 225
Perenyi, Eleanor, 33, 95, 125, 126, 289
Pettingill, Amos, 158
Pfizer, Beryl, 158
Philips, John, 158
Phillpotts, Eden, 289
Planck, Max, 224
Po Chu-I, 260, 261
Polish visitor to Mount Vernon, 33
Politi, Louis, 94
Poncavage, Joanna, 117
Pope, Alexander, 6, 223, 224
Powson, Ernest, 157, 288
Priestly, J. B., 185
Probber, Jonathan, 92
Proust, Marcel, 30, 185
Proverb, Arab, 194
Proverb, Chinese, 1, 12, 92, 142, 260
Proverb, French, 222
Pushkin, Aleksandr, 184

Rand, Edward Sprague, Jr., 183
Ranstu, 156
Rapin, Rene, 92
Raven, Peter H., 287
Raver, Anne, 91, 126, 127, 288
Ray, John, 30, 222
Rayburn, Sam, 222
Reader's Digest Guide to Creative Gardening, 30, 286
Reagan, Ronald, 221
Reese, Lizette Woodworth, 29, 156
Reich, Deborah, 26, 229, 230, 273
Reich, Lee, 91
Renoir, Pierre-Auguste, 191

Richter, Jean Paul, 156
Rickett, Harold William, 221
Riley, James Whitcomb, 286
Rilke, Rainer Maria, 154, 155
Rion, Hanna, 28
Roberts, Cecil, 90
Robinson, William, 90
Rodale, J. I., 127
Rodale's Chemical Free Yard and Garden, 82, 125, 127
Rolland, Romain, 220
Roosevelt, Eleanor, 89
Roosevelt, Theodore, 89
Root, Waverly, 89
Rose, James C., 27
Rosebury, Earl of, Archibald Philip Primrose, 220
Rosenblum, Phyllis, 104, 142
Rossetti, Christina Georgina, 136, 153, 183
Rothery, Agnes, 27, 219
Rousseau, Jean-Jacques, 153
Rumi, Jalaluddin, 219
Ruskin, John, 218, 286

Sackville-West, Vita, 3, 88, 152, 218, 285, 286
Sadi, 26, 134, 136, 253
Saint Exupéry, Antoine de, 264
Saltonstall, Wye, 218
Sand, George, 87, 284, 285
Santayana, George, 217
Sarton, May, 59, 60, 216
Sass, Herbert Ravenel, 10, 138, 215
Schiling, Max, 282
Schuler, Stanley, 86
Scott, Charles, 215
Scott, Geoffrey, 182
Scott, Walter, Sir, 26, 214
Scudder, Vida P., 214
Sedding, John, 26
Semple, Ellen, 213
Serenus, Aulus Septimius, 25, 85
Shaker sister, 280
Shakespeare, William, 82, 83, 150, 151, 152, 181, 212, 213, 250, 280, 281, 282
Shaw, George Bernard, 24, 212

Shelley, Percy Bysshe, 136, 150, 180, 181
Shenstone, William, 24
Shepard, Paul, 211
Sherman, Frank Dempster, 180, 247
Shikibu, Murasaki, 280
Shirley, James, 179
Sibley, Celestine, 122, 123
Silentarus, Paulus, 211
Sitwell, Edith, 122
Sitwell, George, Sir, 23
Smith, A. W., 23
Smith, Alexander, 22, 149, 210
Smith, Charlotte, 22, 209, 279
Smith, Horace, 81, 278
Smith, Martha, 21, 80, 81, 148, 209
Smith, Sheila Kaye, 21
Smythe, F. S., 278
Soifer, Mark, 79
Song of Solomon, verses from, 148, 172, 208
Spalding, John Lancaster, 279
Spencer, Sylvia, 20
Spenser, Edmund, 6, 79, 208, 277
Stein, Gertrude, 276
Stevenson, Adlai E., 207
Stevenson, Robert Louis, 51, 76, 149
Stewart, Martha, 19, 20, 48, 76, 149
Stills, Stephen, 207
Street, Alfred, 206
Stuart, Janet Erskine, 248
Suheili, Anwar-I, 206, 275, 277
Swain, Roger B., 47, 75, 120, 148, 179, 275, 276
Swinburne, Algernon Charles, 135, 147
Swinnerton, Frank, 78
Sydney, Philip, Sir, 146, 205
Sylvester, Michael, 204
Symons, Arthur, 78, 205
Syrus, Publilius, 274

Tabriz, Diwan-I-Shams-I, 274
Tagore, Rabindranath, 120
Tarantino, Rhoda Specht, 19, 47
Taylor, Mary K., 82
Teale, Edwin Way, 120

Temple, William, Sir, 18, 203
Tennyson, Alfred, Lord, 178, 203, 273, 274
Thaxter, Celia, 74, 119, 272, 273
Therest, Saint, 277
Thomas, Dylan, 178, 272
Thomas, Lewis, 118
Thoreau, Henry David, 64, 118, 202, 203, 248, 271
Thurber, James, 100
Tighe, Mary, 271
Toklas, Alice B., 73
Tolstoy, Leo, 146
Tomkins, Peter, 117, 200
Tomlinson, Charles, 269
Torrey, Bradford, 117
Toulet, Paul Jean, 201
Trakl, Georg, 147
Tuckerman, Henry Theodore, 271
Tupper, Martin Farquhar, 73
Tusser, Thomas, 269
Tuwim, Julian, 177
Twain, Mark, 73, 268
Tynan, Katherine, 17, 267, 268

Underhill, Evelyn, 116
Underwood, Loring, 200
Undset, Sigrid, 268
Unknown, 16, 70, 71, 72, 144, 145, 177
Unknown (from Allen's Almanack), 144
Unknown (American farmer, 1842), 268
Unknown (from Farmer's Almanac), 143, 176
Unknown (sixteenth century), 200

Van Doren, Mark, 143
Van Dyke, Henry, 17, 175
Van Gogh, Vincent, 7, 8, 63
Vaughn, William, 265
Verey, Rosemary, 15
Verhaeren, Emile, 15
Verlaine, Paul, 15
Viele-Griffin, Francis, 174
von Goethe, Johann Wolfgang, 200
Von Miklos, Josephine, 16, 115, 142, 199, 265

Von Wifen, Gotfrit, 141

Walker, Alice, 265
Walpole, Horace, 264
Warner, Charles Dudley, 12, 68, 69, 101, 115, 199
Warner, Sam Bass, Jr., 198
Warner, Sylvia Townsend, 115, 265
Washington, George, 198
Watt, James G., 198
Watts, Isaac, 114
Weaver, Lawrence, 281
Webb, Mary, 197
Welsh, Thomas, 263
Westcott, Cynthia, 68
Wharton, Edith, 196
Wheeler, Candace, 196
Wheeler, David, 13
Whistler, James McNeill, 263
White, E. B., 66, 141, 196, 262
White, Gilbert, 102, 103, 104, 105, 111
White, William N., 112, 113
Whiteley, Opal, 262
Whitman, Walt, 13, 194, 195, 262
Whitney, Mrs. A. D. T., 193
Whittier, John Greenleaf, 174, 193, 261, 262
Widdemer, Margaret, 14
Wilberforce, Samuel, 260
Wilde, Oscar, 140, 192, 260, 261
Wilder, Louise Beebe, 14, 67, 259, 260
Wilder, Thornton, 193
Willis, Nathaniel Parker, 140
Wilson, Helen Van Pelt, 66, 67, 259
Winter, Dave, 106
Wodehouse, P. G., 260
Wolfe, Humbert, 14, 258
Wordsworth, Dorothy, 63, 101, 139
Wordsworth, William, 112, 139, 255, 257, 258
Wright, Richardson, 11, 65, 192

Yang, Linda, 11, 65, 256
Yearicks, Gus, 256
Young, Andrew, 174
Yüan Mee, 163

Subject Index

Adam, 83, 210, 223
Agriculture, 25
Air pollution, 61
Allergy sufferers, 199
Almond trees, 129
Aloe, 272
Amaryllis, 169
American gardeners, 59
American gardening, 43
Animals, 100, 109
Anticipation, 37
Ants, 100, 106, 118
Aphids, 102
Apple seeds, 162
Apple trees, 115, 169
Apples, 255
Apricots, 133, 149
April, 129, 144, 158, 160
Arbor Day, 230
Arbours, 33
Arbutus, 134
Art, 26, 211, 214
    fruit trees as form of, 19
    gardening as, 17, 28, 31, 33
    nature as, 217
Artists, 14, 38, 43, 217, 240
    landscape, 44
Ash trees, 172
Asparagus, 56, 57, 252
Asters, 174, 210, 262
August, 168
Autumn, 64, 130, 132, 138, 143, 145, 150, 153, 154, 157, 162–65, 169, 174
Avocados, 89

Back problems, 51, 69, 83, 167
Bartram, John, 282
Basil, 71
Bats, 109
Bays, 70
Bean stalks, 78
Beans, 35
Bears, 121
Beauty, 226, 228
    natural, 21
Beehives, 110
Bees, 28, 101, 106, 110, 114, 122, 126, 293
Beetles, 286
    bean, 102
    flea, 103
    May, 103
    potato, 102
Beets, 74
Birch trees, 262
Birds, 18, 100–2, 105, 107–11, 113, 116–21, 127, 136, 145, 195, *see also* individual names
Blackbirds, 99, 108, 124
Blackcaps, 105
Blossoms, 260, 287, 289
Blue, 291
Bluebells, 244
Blueberries, 175
Bluebirds, 105
Bluejays, 139
Books, 194, 289
Botanical gardens, 38
Botanists, 77, 268
Botany, 284

Boxwood hedges. *See* Hedges
Branches, 84
Breezes, 172, 186, 189
Brown creeper, 117
Buds, 105, 136, 156, 158, 168, 173, 287
Bulbs, 152, 263, 287
Bushes. *See* Shrubbery
Buttercups, 9, 163, 165, 281
Butterflies, 106, 107, 108, 120, 287

Cabbages, 54
Cain, 15
California, 200
Cardinals, 113
Carnations, 68
Carps, 104
Caterpillars, 102
Cauliflower, 73, 90
Central Park garden, 40
Chamise, 292
Cherries, 9, 184
Cherry blossoms, 239
Cherry trees, 5
Chickens, 115
Childhood, 55
Children, 36, 195, 254, 263
Chrysanthemums, 163
City gardeners, 96
City gardens, 11, 21, 34, 196, 198, 256
Civilization, 16, 42, 228, 236
Clothes, 52, 67, 80
Clover, 47, 161, 261
Color, 30, 65, 67, 197, 260, 291
Common sense, 53
Compost, 126
Composting, 52, 96
Concrete cloverleaf, 229
Conservation, 239
Cooking, 51
Corn, 70, 144, 168
Cornfields, 63
Corydalis, 259
Cotoneasters, 85
Cottage gardens, 22, 36

Country gardens, 196
Court of St. James, 99
Cows, 242
Cowslip, 244
Cranberries, 39
Creation, 16, 221, 226, 232, 274
Crickets, 155
Crocuses, 140, 159, 160, 261
Crows, 139
Cuckoo, 244
Cuckoo-buds, 151
Cucumbers, 60, 241
Cupid, 18
Currants, 68
Custodians, 45
Cuttings, 159
Cutworms, 102
Cynic, 232
Cypress trees, 255, 275

Daffodils, 45, 77, 132, 133, 139, 140, 142, 151,
    159, 181, 258, 276
Dahlias, 161
Daisies, 9, 100, 149, 151, 165, 253, 261, 275,
    281
Dandelion wine, 157
Dandelions, 5, 55, 61, 132, 142, 163, 247, 251
Dawn, 87
Daylilies, 164
Daylight, 15
December, 144
Deer, 102, 104, 121
Devon, 202
Dew, 15, 43, 188
Dirt vs. soil, 65
Dogwood, 159
Dreams, 201
Drought, 184, 186
Dust, 62

Earth, 87, 92, 173, 181, 186, 188, 199, 205, 213,
    215, 226, 240, *see also* Soil
Ecosystem, 237
Eden, 27, 35, 39, 191, 203, 217, 223

Eggplant, 90
Eglantine, 132
Elm trees, 274
English gardens, ix–x, 2, 29, 33, 59, 191, 245
Englishmen, 23, 31, 39
Entertaining, 48
Environment, 61, 198, 222, 243, 249
Espalier trees, 162
Eve, 210, 222, 223
Evenings, 109, 117, 124, 129
Evergreens, 166
Exercise, 57

Fairies, 26
Fall. *See* Autumn
Famine, 192
Farmeress, 47
Farmers, 150, 221
Farms, 225, 239
Ferns, 240, 284, 290
Fertilizers, 68, 78, 82
Figs, 149
Finches, 111
Flies, 153
Floods, 186
Florists, 268
Flowers, 1, 4, 12, 18, 23–25, 28, 32, 34, 38, 43,
    47, 51, 63, 66, 67, 70, 74, 78, 81, 84,
    87, 88, 92, 93, 115, 131, 132, 143, 148,
    173, 177, 180, 195, 196, 198, 199, 201,
    205, 206, 211, 216, 220, 222, 227, 229,
    233, 235, 242, 245, 250–52, 254, 257,
    258, 260, 263, 265–67, 271–74,
    276–80, 283, 285–88, 290, 291, 293
  cut, 82
  see also individual names
Foliage, 67
Food, 49, 61, 85, 87, 220, 266
Forest ledge, 22
Fountains, 18, 135
Foxgloves, 64
Fragrance, 4, 22, 27, 64, 87, 134, 205, 242, 244,
    248, 249, 251, 256, 261, 263, 268, 283
Freezes, 186

Friendship, 266
Front yard gardens, 20, 37
Frost, 173, 174, 178, 182, 187, 188
Fruit, 9, 18, 25, 28, 41, 50, 67, 73, 82, 85, 94,
    136, 157, 165, 169, 222, 251, 269, 280,
    282, 291, 293, *see also* individual
    names
Fruit trees, 3, 19, 67, 143, 158, 162, 189, 205,
    213, 217, 261, 270, 274, *see also* indi-
    vidual names

Gamble, 251
Garden, meaning of, 13
Garden clubs, 32
Garden seat, 56
Gardeners, 1, 34, 40, 42, 44, 49, 50, 52, 55, 71,
    72, 78, 80, 83, 87, 92, 164, 186, 199,
    218, 255
  amateur, 84
  American, 59
  city, 96
  death of, 107
  English, 191
  old, 12, 93
Gardening, 4, 10
  American, 43
Gardening records, 95
Gardens:
  city, 11, 21, 34, 196, 198, 256
  cottage, 22, 36
  country, 196
  English, ix–x, 2, 29, 33, 59, 191, 245
  front yard, 20, 37
  herb, 47
  ideal, 68
  Italian, 258
  Japanese, 194
  kitchen, 17
  poor man's, 32
  public, 8
  see also Vegetable gardens
Gardens of Babylon, 17
Garlic, 66
Gates, garden, 14, 15

German weed, 57
God, 15, 24, 27, 30, 37, 39, 100, 169, 171, 174,
        195, 201, 203, 205, 208, 210, 227, 229,
        231, 260, 263, 274
Goldenrod, 174, 210, 262
Goldfinches, 117
Gooseberries, 68
Grain, 176
Grapefruit, 281
Grapes, 25, 85
Grass, 10, 47, 100, 112, 160, 166, 169, 194,
        195, 206, 216, 232, 234, 240, 257, 274
Grasshoppers, 106
Greenhouses, 5, 219
Greens, 25
Grouse, 121
Groves, citrus, 51

Habits, 21
Happiness, 12
    pursuit of, 210
Hardy plants, 73
Harvest, 164
Hay, 144
Hazels, 85
Health, 15
    garden, 70
Hearts Ease, 171
Heather, 141
Heaven, 11, 39, 69, 112
Hedges, 13, 42, 153, 196, 233, 256
Heliotrope, 261
Hepatica, 285
Herb garden, 47
Herbalist, 241
Herbicides, 91, 124
Herbs, 25, 28, 41, 64, 71, 85, 96, 100, 171, 201,
        233, 250, 266, 268, 274, 284
Herimone, 252
Hiding places, 14
History, 269
Holly, 70, 85
Hollyhock, 226
Honeysuckle, 133

Hope, 186
Horticulture, 31, 33, 52, 95, 250
Hoses, 90, 107
Hostas, 240, 284
Houses, old, 13
Hyacinth, 141, 271, 283
Hybrid witch, 85

Ideal garden, 68
Imagination, 16
Impatience, 55
Insect control. See Pest control
Insecticides, 103
Insects, 82, 103, 104, 106, 108, 110, 112–15,
        117, 120, 122, 125, see also Pests;
        individual names
Irises, 11, 151, 160, 245
Italian gardens, 258
Ivy, 70, 214, 254, 267, 281

Japanese gardens, 194
Jasmine, 2, 68, 261, 275
Jewelweed, 178
Jujobes, 85
June, 132, 140, 168
Juniper, 77, 262

Kitchen gardens, 17
Knees, your, 70
Knucklebones, 39

Labeling, plant, 91
Ladybugs, 124
Lady-smocks, 151
Land, 61, 216, 226
Landscape, 192, 196, 202, 206
    natural, 239
Landscape artist, 232
Landscaping, 7, 12, 36, 39, 44, 48, 57, 74, 77,
        86, 208, 241, 290
Laurel, 70
Lavender, 150, 267
Lawnmowers, 155

Lawns, 4, 58, 78, 234
Leaves, 28, 150
Legumes, 92
Lettuce, 56
Library, 1
Life, 6, 40
    beginning of, 1
    cycles of, 267
Lilacs, 14, 17, 167, 250, 262, 292
Lilies, 3, 9, 35, 41, 79, 122, 132, 142, 151, 270,
    271, 277, 285
Love, 20, 29, 38, 49, 240, 245, 260, 266, 268,
    277, 280, 282
Lovers, 220, 231
Lupins, 286

Magic, 8
Magnolias, 255, 285
Manure, 66, 87, 96
Manzanita, 292
March, 143
Marigolds, 150, 157, 267, 293
Marjoram, 150
Markets, 10
Masterpiece, 263
Maude, 203
May, 144, 168
Meadows, 66, 263
Meditation, 12, 18, 19, 22, 30
Memories, 131
Mignotte, 261
Mint, 150, 266
Mist, 181
Mistletoe, 39
Monet's garden, 30
Moon, 2, 172, 202, 228
Moon shine, 186
Morning glory, 13
Mornings, 43, 120
Moss, 2, 137, 206
Muck-worm, 112
Muscles, your, 81
Mushrooms, 53
Music, 18

Names, plant, 90, 292
National flower, 229
National preserves, 200
Natural gardens, 278
Natural resources, 89
Nature, 10, 69, 91, 97, 118, 148, 188, 197, 199,
    201, 203, 205, 208, 211, 213, 214, 217,
    222, 243, 269
    mystery of, 224
Neighbor's gardens, 17
Nettles, 281
Newspapers, 198
Night, 87
Nightingale, 119
Nights, summer, 145
November, 129

Oak trees, 209, 214, 243, 269
Oranges, 277
Orchards, 50, 189
Orchids, 183
Orioles, 167
Osiers, 145

Painting, 191
Pampas grass, 77
Paradise, 1, 26, 159, 212
Parks, 200
Pathways, 10, 45, 197, 206, 232, 262, 288
Patience, 55, 222, 248
Peace, 264
Peaches, 48, 73, 149
Pear trees, 244, 274
Pears, 248
Peonies, 40, 244, 245, 254
Peppers, 49
Perennials, 292
Periwinkle, 288
Pest control, 99, 100, 101, 103, 113, 114,
    123
    natural, 125
Pesticides, 68, 123
Pests, 68, 101, 102, 104, 125, 127
Peter Collinson's garden, 39

Philosophy, 3, 13, 15, 18, 21, 23–25, 27, 29, 40, 54, 60, 62, 67, 68, 69, 72, 75, 78–81, 83–85, 87, 88, 92, 97, 105, 117, 125, 126, 134, 135, 142, 145, 146, 150, 151, 153, 155–57, 161, 164, 166, 169, 184, 187, 188, 192–200, 202, 203, 205–40, 242, 243, 245, 248, 250, 255, 259, 264, 265, 268, 269, 271, 278, 279, 282, 283, 286–91
Phlox, 161
Physical labor, 95
Pig weed, 57
Pine trees, 134, 141, 227, 236
Planets, 28
Plant sculpture, 26
Planter's Paralysis, 81
Plows, 218
Poor man's garden, 32
Poplar trees, 263
Poppies, 11, 161, 177, 179, 279
Porcupines, 102
Posies, 291
Potato plants, 63
Potatoes, 92, 95, 262, 278, 287
Prairies, 7, 209
Primrose, 131, 253, 288
Primrose paths, 10
Prison, 23
Propagation, 264, 288
Proverbs, 1, 12, 92, 142, 194, 222, 233, 260
Pruning, 52, 191
Pruning shears, 95
Public gardens, 8
Pumpkin patch, 48
Purslane, 57

Quack grass, 57
Queen Anne's Lace, 164

Raccoons, 102
Radishes, 142
Rag grass, 77
Rain, 171, 174, 181, 188, 210
    showers, 66, 175, 177, 180
    storm, 176

Redwood trees, 221
Reptiles, 109
Rivers, 11, 135, 205
Robins, 107, 111, 139
    redbreast, 101
Rocks, 229
Roots, 86, 87
Rosemary, 70, 266, 273
Roses, 2, 3, 9, 17, 20, 27, 35, 41, 68, 75, 76, 79, 94, 104, 131, 132, 139, 141, 142, 145, 146, 153, 161, 162, 164, 184, 185, 209, 218, 235, 249, 254–56, 261, 262, 264, 271, 276–80, 283, 285, 291

Sage, 266
Sanctuary, 19, 22, 24, 26, 32, 38, 59, 66, 89, 97, 179, 204, 209, 228, 237
Saviour, 23
Savories, 71
Savory, 150
Scent. *See* Fragrance
Scrub oak, 292
Sculpture, 27
Seasons, 135, 141, 149, 153, 161, *see also* individual names
Secret Garden, 179
Seed catalogues, 130, 148, 275
Seeds, 28, 136, 248, 252, 253, 258, 273, 274, 276, 287, 290
Senses, 3, 21, 27, 28, 76
September, 155, 163
Shade, 18, 41, 85
Shakespeare garden, 196
Shape, garden, 39
Sheep, 121
Shells, 272
Shelter, 85
Shelters, garden, 14
Shoes, 67
Shrubbery, 10, 30, 57, 85, 263, 288
Size, garden, 19, 37
Sky, 145, 173, 232
Slugs, 83, 116, 118, 119
Snow, 151, 167, 171, 174, 179, 184, 185
Snowdrops, 138, 178

Soil, 47, 62, 63, 65, 69, 87, 91, 127, 130, 134, 222, 236, 238
Solitude, 233
Sombre fir, 262
Sorrel, 77
Sourwoods, 85
Sowing, 72
Sparrows, 167
Spiders, 101
Spirit renewal, 21
Spring, 129–31, 133–39, 141, 142, 144–48, 150–52, 154, 156, 157, 159–63, 167, 169, 257
Squirrels, 105
Stars, 23, 174
Stein, Gertrude, 73
Stones, 250
Storms, 182
Strawberries, 83, 184, 247, 253
Strawberry beds, 68
Streams, 11, 135, 229
Summer, 130, 132, 137, 141, 142, 146, 148, 150, 151, 162, 165
Summer days, 177
Sun, 176
Sunshine, 171, 173, 174, 179, 184, 206, 210, 244
Swallows, 106, 111, 126, 132
Swamp, 112
Sycamore trees, 214
Sympathy, 203

Tarragon, 96
Terriers, 141
Thames River, 36
Thorns, 75, 76
Thrushes, 108, 132
Thumb, brown, 65
Thyme, 71, 266, 286
Tibet, 77
Time, 227, 233
    availability of, 53
Toad, 101
Tomatoes, 74, 90, 97, 142
    cherry, 94

Tools, 71
Topiary art, 280
Tortoise, 103
Tree of Life, 231
Trees, 10, 28, 47, 56, 66, 73, 85, 105, 116, 134, 145, 149, 176, 191–93, 195–98, 203, 206, 211, 212, 214, 216, 222, 224, 227–31, 236, 238, 243, 244, 248, 257, 279
    flowering, 261
    see also Fruit trees; individual names
Truth, 26
Tulip trees, 214
Tulips, 156, 158, 254, 275, 292
Turkeys, 123
Twilight, 29

Ultexes, 85
Unicorn, 100
Urns, 13

Vegetable gardening, 49, 104
Vegetable gardens, 16, 56, 57, 90, 95, 262
Vegetables, 41, 50, 51, 62, 68, 74, 85, 93, 97, 109, 115, 181, 265, see also individual names
Vines, 10, 200
Violets, 54, 105, 125, 130, 132, 137, 151, 160, 169, 275, 284
Virginia creeper, 255
Vistas, 207

Wake-robin, 132
Wasps, 110
Water, 69, 222, 286
Watering, 60, 89, 94
Weather, 175, 184, 185
    bad, 188
    see also individual types of
Weedkillers, 108
Weeds, 10, 26, 47, 48, 55, 57, 60, 62, 69, 73, 77, 79, 82, 84, 90, 91, 94, 97, 115, 124, 187, 201, 247
White House Rose Garden, 17

Wilderness, 3, 204
Wildflowers, 72, 133, 272
Wildlife, 109, 121
Willows, 138
Wind, 171–73, 177, 180, 182, 183, 185, 186, 198, *see also* Breezes
Wine, 153
Winter, 136, 137, 139, 140, 144, 147–50, 158, 162, 164, 167, 178, 182
Woodbine, 14, 132, 209

Woodchucks, 102, 103, 122
Woodlands, 147
Woodthrush, 108, 132
Woody plants, 85, 86
Worms, 107
Wrens, 139
Writers, 289

Zen gardens, 12
Zucchini, 60